TIED TOGETHER
a Pathway to Hope

WAYNE ELSEY AND **MELISSA ELSEY PITTS**

D1570034

WEE PUBLISHING
ORLANDO

Published by WEE Publishing

1080 Woodcock Rd, S-151, Orlando, FL 32803

ISBN: 978-0-578-48629-1

DEDICATION

To everyone, as we all Matter, we all are one world one people, ONE.

To my partner and the love of my life, Courtney. **YOU Matter!**

To my favorite daughter (oh, I only have one) Melissa and her patient, awesome husband, Josh. **YOU Matter.**

To my three favorite grandchildren (yes, I'm that old) Aubree, Aiden, and Jaxon who inspired me to write the book. **YOU Matter.**

To my critics – **YOU Matter** also!

To the hundreds of folks that endorsed the book, thanks for being part of the tribe and in my life through the years. **YOU Matter.**

To all the people who I may have forgotten or met, even for a moment.

YOU MATTER.

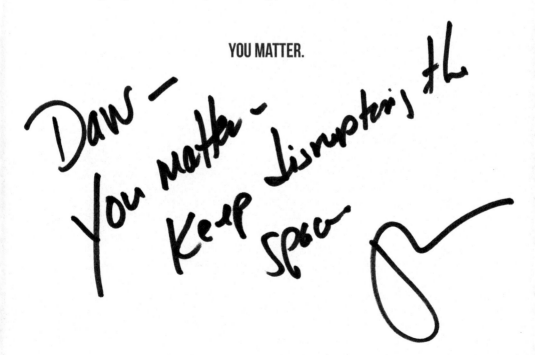

TABLE OF CONTENTS

ENDORSEMENTS

"Wayne Elsey, whose life's ethos is 'YOU Matter,' has written a must-read book for anyone looking to create a business and also make a social impact." – **Dan Pallotta**

"This book is a thoughtful look at what it really means to be human and how we all have more in common than we realize. Wayne has led the way as a social entrepreneur, setting an example of what's possible when we understand that we are all in this together." – **Jeff Goins, bestselling author of *The Art of Work***

"Wayne Elsey has written a must-read for anyone considering philanthropy....Read this book and learn from one of the best." – **Teri Griege, Founder & President, Powered by Hope**

"Wayne Elsey is the king of inspiring individuals to believe in themselves enough to make a difference. His organizations have been serving the very least fortunate among us for almost twenty years. His new book *Tied Together: A Pathway to Hope* gives readers the courage to create extraordinary incomes and to improve lives at the most basic levels around the world." – **Keith Landry, former TV News Anchor, Orlando, FL**

"The theme of 'Knight Rider,' a television show in which I starred alongside David Hasselhoff, was 'One man can make a difference.' Wayne Elsey is the embodiment of that statement, and in his new book, *Tied Together: A Pathway to Hope,* he shares his roadmap for doing so and inspires us all to find a way to make it our life theme as well. This book makes the perfect Christmas gift! Wayne's inspirational message and his generosity of spirit are what the holidays are all about." – **Rebecca Holden**

"In a world of political turmoil with death and destruction everywhere, where truth and human experience are lost comes a book of hope and assurance that inspires us to see the best of life. *Tied Together: A Pathway to Hope* is a book that the whole world should read. It should be in every school and church. It would be a great gift for young and old, i.e., for those graduating from high school or college, it would be a guide book for life's choices. I am an associate professor of education. I am donating copies to my university's library, my church library, and my grandchildren. Inspiring. Feel better book." – **Jackie Smith Busch, Ph.D.**

"I feel truly blessed to have the opportunity to be connected via a strong personal friendship and business partnership with such a phenomenal individual as Wayne Elsey. Wayne is the essence of a magnetic personality and has a passion for creating positive impacts with everyone he encounters. This book, *Tied Together: A Pathway to Hope,* is a great opportunity for the world to gain valuable insight from Wayne's successes and the corresponding experiences that helped yield those results. Wayne is a generational leader that has both the heart to identify essential needs within communities across the world and the vision and business acumen to be able to execute strategies to implement a solution." – **Matthew Freimuth, Vice President, Regional Corporate Banking, BB&T**

"*Tied Together: A Pathway to Hope* is an inspirational challenge to all of us. Wayne Elsey walks us through stages to examine the world as it is today and act upon our passions to create a lasting hope for generations. If you are searching for practical advice based on proven success on how to change the world around you, this is the book to read." – **Tony DiFranco, NonProfit Marketing Entrepreneur and Awesomeness Innovator**

"It's one thing to say that you want to heal the brokenness of the world and make it a better place. It's quite another thing to think you can actually pull it off. We get so pre-occupied with the size of the herculean task and give up before we even start. On December 26, 2004, Wayne Elsey discovered that to change the world, it didn't mean making it better for the seven-plus billion who inhabit our planet. Bettering the life of just one person was enough to start a chain reaction of hope. Wayne has impacted tens of millions of people around the world with his unfailing desire to simply be more for others, and he is living proof that what you want, and what you think, are not mutually exclusive." – **Dan Duffy, Co-Founder, The Half Fund**

"What a breath of fresh air! Wayne's latest book is a hopeful departure from the divisive noise permeating our lives today. *Tied Together: A Pathway to Hope* puts the focus back on all the things that unite us as humans.

It will leave you inspired to live that impactful life you've long envisioned. One person can make a difference, and this book will show you how."
– **Stacy Case, Former CBS News National Correspondent, Fox Nashville Main Anchor, Murrow & Emmy Award Winning Journalist, 26 Year News Veteran**

"Wayne Elsey is a gem among men. A heart so big it could never be contained to family, friends, and colleagues alone. Wayne's reach of love and care was meant to extend to the world at large. His drive to not only help but to empower the less fortunate or those struck by disaster is a privilege to witness. His ability to infuse being in service with a sense of playfulness and dignity for everyone involved is astounding. The greatest food for the soul. I am proud to call Wayne my friend and will always hold our time in Haiti together as an example of the goodness of humanity. The very thing Wayne is gifted to see clearly in others." – **Caroline Diaco, President/Publisher, Footwear Plus Magazine**

"When I think about my incredibly business savvy, freely-giving friend, Wayne Elsey, one word comes to mind: philanthropreneur. Every single day, Wayne makes it his mission to lend a helping hand up, to create opportunities in his work environment, in his community and globally. It's an honor to be a part of his world and a blessing to watch the powerful impact he makes everywhere." – **Ted Bogert, Creator and Host, The Ted Show**

"Wayne Elsey understands what it means to ACT! There are many people who talk about doing this or doing that, but Wayne understands the importance of putting words into action."– **Dave Bratcher, President, STAR Center Inc.**

"Wayne Elsey is the epitome of a person who shows you just how well he can do what you told him could not be done. His knack for creative thinking and problem solving, with his genuine interest in helping others, it makes him one of my favorite people with whom to work—he's an inspiring source of professional and personal insights for audiences ranging from new-to-the-sector to those of us who need a reminder of why we do what we do." – **Amy DeVita, COO, TopNonprofits**

"Wayne's inspiring strategies and leadership are at the forefront of this book. He continues to color outside of the lines and has the enthusiasm that fosters confidence and trust from the people in his tribe. It's a fascinating and thought-provoking read for anyone in the social good sector." – **Adam Weinger, President, Double the Donation**

"Wayne is an enthusiastic, incredibly empathetic person. His vision for helping others is unmatched, whether it's the impoverished people in poorer countries he's never even met or the people working for him on that mission. He will roll up his sleeves and do the dirty work alongside you, help you in any way to further the cause. Wayne cares most about the human connection and uplifting each other. I hope many people find the inspiration they need to make a difference in *Tied Together: A Pathway to Hope*." – **Timothy Rasmussen b/k/a $hamrock, Vh1/MTV personality, national recording artist & songwriter.**

"Wayne Elsey has proven, yet again, why he is a true visionary! This new book sets the stage for growing humanity in each of us while offering a glimpse into how Head2Toe Recycling will act as an unmatched agent for helping provide the most basic of life's needs." – **Chris Lyons, Publisher, NonProfit PRO**

FOREWORD

We live in a world where, for many, it is their differences that define them, rather than their similarities. Where the separation between different beliefs, creates a divide between countries, communities, and even friends.

We exist in a world where, increasingly, people feel as if the rope that ties together all humanity is becoming frayed.

Sometimes, we need a reminder. A reminder that instead of a fraying rope, there does exist a strong bond, by which, we as a people do exist, and that within us all is the seed to be more, and to do more.

Wayne Elsey gives us this reminder in *Tied Together: A Pathway to Hope*.

This book arrives at the perfect time, by which we can individually, and collectively awaken — awaken to manifest the highest potential for ourselves and our world.

I have spent over thirty years in the footwear and apparel industry, starting on the retail side, and eventually being fortunate enough to manage some of the most iconic footwear brands ever created.

For Wayne to "just" have a successful career in the footwear industry, it would have been enough. As a leading industry executive, he would have been respected, traveled to great cities, eaten at great restaurants, and after many years of planting seeds, he would have harvested a good life.

But some people hear a different calling. Wayne left the "footwear industry" only to create his OWN "industry"—one where he used all his years of industry knowledge, inside connections, strong relationships, and coupled them with something almost previously unheard of—the idea of social entrepreneurship.

He went from "feet on the ground" at an industry trade show, to "feet on the ground" helping people on the dirt streets of Haiti.

Sure, many "talk" about "doing good," but how many, actually jump off the corporate treadmill, only to create their own treadmill—where they do good, by what they do every day—where the social element of giving back, of empowering others, is not separate from the mission; it IS the mission? Wayne's first enterprise Soles4Souls embodied a higher calling and came at the time of some of the greatest natural disasters in history—and in some cases, where Wayne's efforts may have been the only path to hope for some of those affected.

Here, Wayne shares lessons from that experience. A lot of what worked. And even some that didn't. Understanding the business side is just half of the equation. Realizing what he took from this experience, to create what is now the next generation model of social entrepreneurialism, and for-profit social enterprises, and how he developed personally as well as professionally is what lays the groundwork for the wisdom he now shares.

Wayne says, "We can be better. We can do better," and he challenges us to think differently. He asks us, "Do you think we can do better for each other?" It would be easy to wake up, go to work every day, come home, flip on the TV, go to bed, and fall deeper and deeper into the haze that now is becoming more prevalent—a malaise that continually harps on the differences between people, rather than the shared humanity. Unfortunately, having a "fear" based mentality creates limited thinking and pulls each of us, further apart, rather than closer together.

Tied Together: A Pathway to Hope reminds us that we are all part of the same tribe—we are all part of human-kind. And the one quality we share above all else is hope.

It is the hope for a better way to serve those in need that has driven Wayne for the past 20 years. It is the hope that he could create a new business model that combines FOR-PROFIT dynamics with a FOR GOOD mindset. It is the hope that he can take what HE has experienced and impact others so they may take bold actions to impact and best serve others. It is the hope that there exists in each of us the same spark that ignited Wayne to take action.

Wayne's lessons aren't the stuff of some armchair quarterback or academic. As an entrepreneur, he has taken the bold steps himself, he has practiced, what he preaches, and we are now, the beneficiaries of his unique insights.

David Kahan
Chief Executive Officer
Birkenstock Americas
San, Rafael, CA

PREFACE

"A small group of thoughtful people could change the world.
Indeed, it's the only thing that ever has."
— Margaret Mead

Not too long ago I found myself sitting with my daughter, her husband and my three grandchildren who were playing. As I sat there watching the little ones, what came to mind is how incredibly fortunate I am in my life to have such a beautiful family. As I reflected a couple of days later on time spent with my daughter, her husband, and the grandchildren, I also thought about the many kids I saw who were growing up in developing nations, and right here in our own country, who lacked some of the most basic things in their young lives for a healthy childhood.

I thought of the young teen I met once who was wearing sneakers that were being held together with duct tape. It turns out they were his only pair and were two sizes too small because his single mother could not afford another pair for him. I reflected on the son of one of the micro-entrepreneurs (small business owners) I've partnered with in my work, Silvia, who will soon be graduating college because of his mother's determination not to allow poverty to ruin the opportunity for an education for her son. You'll learn more about their story later in the book. And, I thought about another mother in a developing nation who was so impoverished that she gave away her only shoes in exchange for a goat so she could feed her baby. Some of the stories are heartbreaking, and yet, often uplifting because you can feel the love and courage of the human spirit.

My daughter, Melissa, and I have had plenty of conversations along the way about my work, and she saw a lot of what I was doing when she was growing up in my home. Some of the comments she's made, as have other people in her age group, have been about paying it forward. My daughter, who's a Millennial, happens to be one of my greatest champions, and although admittedly I know she's biased in her view of my entrepreneurial and humanitarian work, I've been humbled by her faith in me and also others who have asked me to share what I've learned.

A Shift in Direction

It's been a while since I wrote a book, but since that day in Melissa and Josh's living room, I've started to get an old feeling that I have more to say. However, unbeknownst to me when I began writing, this particular book would become a labor of love. The deadlines my team and I set for the publication of the book came and went, which was fine because the book became so much more than the words that were written within its pages. As my team and I were moving toward production, we invited people to share some of their thoughts, never realizing that my request would become proof of the incredible people who have crossed my path at different points through my life. The outpouring of sentiment changed the tone and the tenor of the book.

What started as a book that would explain what my team and I accomplished in the aftermath of the 2004 Indian Ocean tsunami to how my current team and I have been able to create brands that make a global impact and profit became a re-affirmation of what Margaret Mead said in the quote mentioned at the beginning of this preface.

During the holidays, I was flooded with endorsements, shared memories and reflections. Candidly, I was incredibly moved by the outpouring and shared observations about how others view the impact my teams and I have made. However, as much of a blessing as dozens of pages of thoughts from so many was in my life, and the fact that I learned firsthand what others thought about what I had done with my teams, I realized I had a challenge. While the positive support and inspirations were humbling and amazing, the tone of the book had shifted. Because I know that nothing that I've ever achieved has been accomplished without the support and people who have shared in the visions, I needed to shift the focus of this book away from what could be viewed as my accomplishments to what others and I have done.

I spent weeks wondering how to proceed forward with the book, even as my team tried to nudge me along to keep to its publication deadline, which we missed. I realized I had something extraordinary on my hands, and I needed to honor what people wrote and believed.

I remember sitting at my desk at home staring at the printed pages of the book I had so far in one pile and another with 40 pages of additional material that people sent to me in support of my work and life. Somehow, I knew I had to join together what I had written with the 40 pages of words from so many other people who wanted to voice their support or express their thoughts on the work or experiences I had shared with them.

During the holidays, when I spent the time with the people I most loved in the world, including my wife, Courtney, Melissa, Josh, and my three grandchildren, Aubree, Aiden and Jaxon, I continued to marinate in my mind the direction of the book. I spoke to my family and as always happens if you're patient, with the passing of the days, I had an answer, which was offered to me by Courtney. After seeing the notes and knowing how much I care about Melissa and her kids, she suggested that I ask Melissa to co-author the book with me. As Courtney knew, Melissa has been a motivating force in my life ever since the day she was born and everything I've ever done since that day has been to make her, and now my grandchildren, proud.

I listened to what Courtney had to say, for the first time (smile), mulled it over for a few days and then asked Melissa. She agreed to co-author this book with me, and it's something that makes me immensely honored because she's always meant the world to me. And now, with her own family, she and I had an opportunity to create something and leave a legacy together that will hopefully capture a bit of the spirit of how we both live our lives—fully and in service to others.

The book that you're reading today is distinctly different in color and flavor from what I originally wrote because of the voices of so many others throughout the pages. I'm humbled and appreciative of all the people who shared endorsements, memories, and stories. I hope that the reworked book, now with Melissa as a co-author, will inspire and demonstrate that each one of us matters and that, together, a small group of dreamers and doers can change the world.

Tied Together

The reality is that we seem to live in a divided world and nation. People have gotten more entrenched in the division and talking past each other. It's not only something that is happening just in our great country, but it is also occurring around the world. If you read the news or watch it on television on any given day, it's a litany of anger, division, and a whole lot of drama and self-righteousness. If you're on social media, more than likely you've had someone on Facebook or Twitter trying to challenge you negatively. I've got my dedicated group of trolls and critics!

However, there are many people as well who are saying that we can do better and be better. We have leaders young and old who are raising their voices and saying that we have to see the humanity in each other, and it begins with respect and listening. I think we can do better, and I know Melissa does as well because doing our part to leave a better world than what we've each found for future generations is what we should all aspire to do as we pass through this world. I want to be better, and I guess that you do as well. We can each play a part in helping to create a world where we all respect and listen to each other and try to make it a better place. There is so much need out there and so much that we can do for each other to help our families, communities, and others around the planet. When you think about it, we're all tied together as human beings.

Love, Fear, and Hope

Have you ever thought about our collective humanness? I have. These days it seems that we're missing the point on what binds us, and we focus almost exclusively on what divides us. For instance, I don't know about you, but every human being that I've ever met wants acceptance. Deep down, they want someone to appreciate and care about them, and they want to care about others.

I think it's also fair to say that every human being can experience fear. None of us are characters in a big-budget action film where we are utterly fearless in the face of any catastrophe that may be happening. Even those of us who demonstrate a lot of bravery and courage are afraid of something, be it a health concern, loss of our family or friends or even something like the fear of speaking in public. I don't know any person who does not have some element of fear in his or her human experience; do you? As I always say, there's a natural disaster happening in someone's life every day, and each one of us walks a journey that—hopefully—builds character, experience and the attributes that make us uniquely human.

Still, stepping out and doing something requires that you step out of your comfort zone, which causes fear and may bring you critics, but doing so offers the potential of more extraordinary returns and rewards.

An essential aspect of being human is our connection to the value of HOPE. It is the hope for a better future that keeps us striving forward, taking risks and overcoming our fears to improve our well-being, as well as that of our families, communities, and even the world. I have a question for you: Do you think we can do and be better for each other? If you agree with me that the answer is yes, then we share a hope that the world will be better—not just for some of us, but for all of us. I, for one, hope that the world will be a safer, cleaner and a more beautiful place for my three grandchildren. I hope they will grow to ripe old ages, have seen brilliant colors in their world, and have experienced little rain in their lives. But even when they do have a few storms in their lives, I hope that it will strengthen their characters and make them even more grateful for the good times.

Paying it Forward

I think my generation has an extraordinary opportunity in this day and age. We know what the world was like before technology entered into most of our homes—where a phone was connected to a cord and a wall and not something we carried wherever we went. Years of experience, in fact, does bring wisdom, one hopes. But it also brings insights about how to get from an idea developed around a kitchen table to a multi-million enterprise seeking to help organizations, people around the world and the environment.

What can my team and I offer to others who want to follow our path? We can share what's worked and what hasn't. We can provide context and history, based on experience, of the social issues that humans face. And, we can serve as a bridge for the others who are seeking to change the world as we know it for the better.

That brings me to what you, the reader, will learn and discover. Melissa and I aim to pay it forward. I will share with you the experiences that my teams and I have had in our social entrepreneurial and humanitarian work into the pages of this book. I also want to share with you some of the realities people around the world face so that perhaps, it can inspire you to pick up and join us in doing something about it. I'd love to hear, in the coming years, your solutions and ideas about how to address the intractable challenges that have plagued the world. In my conversations speaking to Melissa, once she became the co-author of this book, she expressed her desire to help add context to what many of the people have written in support of the work my teams and I have done. Again, nothing I've ever accomplished have I done alone. It's always been with the efforts of committed and thoughtful people who have joined me on the ride.

A Pathway to Hope

This book will be divided into two parts. The first part of the book will be divided into three sections. In the first section, I will tell you how I came to become a social entrepreneur both in the nonprofit and for-profit sectors. My story in becoming a humanitarian activist and social entrepreneur began on December 26, 2004. Although I've written about some of my experiences in my earlier book *Almost Isn't Good Enough*, I want to share with you additional thoughts, including the lessons learned, because what I have now to share has the distance of time and years as a social entrepreneur. At this point, I've been a social entrepreneur for many years. I will reflect on what worked at the nonprofit I founded, Soles4Souls, what didn't and most importantly—why.

The second section of the first part of the book will serve to inspire you, at least that's what I hope. I understand that many people have it tough, and even you, the reader, may be thinking that your life isn't all about rainbows. But, I want to tell you some of the stories of the people my team and I have met because they speak to the human spirit, and hopefully will help you realize that we're all in this thing called life together. Not a day passes where I am not personally inspired by others to stretch and do more. Each person matters. YOU Matter.

The reality is that it was the stories of the people I met, who hoped for a better life, that kept me going when I resigned Soles4Souls, which was the nonprofit I founded after decades in the footwear industry. Although I soon established str@tegic,[1] which is focused on strategic planning, marketing, and branding, my mind regularly drifted to the idea of how to continue to make a humanitarian impact in the world and implement it in a way that made sense. Because I was open to figuring out how to help and listening to others, things started to come together reasonably quickly.

The deeper my team and I got into the work with str@tegic, the more we realized that nonprofits were also in great need of funding, which is why the for-profit social enterprise I founded, Funds2Orgs, was established. While I was growing str@tegic, I was also getting calls from people in developing countries who were looking to purchase unwanted and used shoes from the U.S. so they can sell them in their communities. At the time, they would tell me that inventory had dried up and they needed more product to market. If they didn't have the product, they didn't make money, so obtaining merchandise was of vital interest.

It was at that point that I put two and two together and saw the connection between the need of nonprofits for a creative way to raise money and that of people in developing nations looking for footwear inventory so they can sell the shoes and have a sustainable income amid systemic poverty. That awareness became the driving force and reason why I founded my first for-profit social enterprise with a great group of believers who wanted to make the world a better place with Funds2Orgs, which I'll explain further in Chapter 2.

For now, suffice to say that it was the knowledge that although our race, gender, faith, language, citizenship or experiences are different, we are all still the same in many ways, and that has kept my team and I focused on creating opportunities for as many people as possible around the world. Nonprofits serve those in need in their communities. In the meantime, micro-entrepreneurs in developing nations need economic paths out of poverty. We also need to leave the planet healthier than we found it,

---

1 Website: http://elseyenterprises.com/

TIED TOGETHER: A PATHWAY TO HOPE

and that means limiting what goes into landfills and extending the life of textiles, such as shoes or clothing. Couple those elements with my interest in the challenge of developing successful businesses as an entrepreneur, I realized my team and I could make a broad social impact, tackling multiple issues.

You'll learn how my team and I refined and perfected our thinking based on experience to develop what is now known as Funds2Orgs Group,[2] which accomplishes four benefits for society. You'll also discover what my team and I have done as we've prepared to launch a new brand, Head2Toe Recycling.[3] All of this can be useful for you and serve as a roadmap if you're interested in creating your own for-profit social enterprise.

In the second part of the book, my daughter, Melissa, will pick up the narrative and share her thoughts and insights to put the reflections and stories I received from people in my life into context. I think Melissa's impressions will add perspective to the submissions from others. Again, any one of us can change someone else's life, and sometimes that happens without our ever realizing it.

If you've ever thought about making a positive difference, even a global one beyond your local community, I'm here to tell you that you can do it. One person, or a small group of thoughtful and committed people, can make a difference.

Let's work together to create a better world. Join my team and me, and so many others, in looking at the world a little differently for yourself and others by remaining positive in spite of those who want to divide us, ignoring the critics, being a better version of yourself each day, and making an impact.

---

2 Website: https://mailchi.mp/funds2orgs.com/rethinkfundraising
3 Website: https://head2toerecycling.com/

INTRODUCTION

"If you want to go fast, go alone. If you want to go far, go together."
— *African Proverb*

We are all tied together whether it is by jobs, family, experiences or even relationships. When thinking of who I am tied together with, the first characteristic that comes to mind is, family.

When my dad asked me to join him in co-authoring this book with him, initially I wasn't sure how it would come together. Yes, it's a bit of irony that I couldn't immediately figure out how it would all get "tied together." But, the more I listened to my dad and learned about the response he had received from people who contributed thoughts about him and his work, I knew that somehow we would make it work. It's always about family, and I knew that we could eventually make anything come together.

It's fun to think of a dad who encouraged me to get on a bike as a kid while he was on another bicycle at Toys "R" Us as we rode unendingly around the store until managers told us to buy a bike or leave them behind because it was closing time. And, then I juxtapose those memories with the professional who is Wayne Elsey, the founder and CEO of Elsey Enterprises—a global suite of businesses and brands.

The experiences that he has had throughout his career, in my view and many others, can be classified as undoubtedly breathtaking and one of a kind. He's a man who believes firmly that anything, and I mean *anything*, is possible. He's also someone who thinks in his heart that everyone matters. As those who follow his work know, his personal tagline is "YOU Matter." I can tell you that he's been living that way since as long as I can remember.

My dad is committed to making a difference in the world, and while he has done just that, he's not finished. Yes, I am proud of the millions of shoes collected, which have ultimately gone to those in need over his career. How awesome is that? But, he's someone that is never satisfied, and there's always more to get done. Somehow, he's also been able to inspire not only those of us who personally know him to join him in his ventures, but he's even touched the lives of people whom he has met for a moment or those who have been with him in some way on the journey of his life and work.

My father is committed, as a business entrepreneur, to make a difference in the world, understanding that even a pair of shoes can change someone's life. I'm proud of the fact that my children, Aubree, Aiden, and Jaxon, have someone in their lives, aside from their father and me, who encourages them to dream, dare, believe—and hope. Even though he's someone who loves laughs and fun, he's serious about his work. All of what he's done with his teams throughout the years have become a reality with tireless amounts of hard work, dedication, and perseverance. It's been that drive and focus that has brought him, and so many others, success and why the people who share his life or work worlds are continually charged, reinvigorated and believing in the art of the possible.

Tied Together as a Family

My husband and I have three beautiful children, Aubree (5), Aiden (3) and Jaxon (1). They're the light of our lives and our daily inspiration even in times of chaos.

I mentioned that my dad's philosophy is "YOU Matter." Those words begin at home. When I was a child, I remember my dad taking me to get a professional foot massage. Fast forward, and my dad has done it with my daughter, Aubree. In this instance, like her grandfather, Aubree wants regular foot massages now.

The family is at the core of everything my dad does in his life. Every single morning at 8:00 AM before he starts his day, he calls the kids to sing with them. The first time he called, the kids were excited, and they sang loud and proud on the phone. But, as happens with kids, by the fifth and sixth day, they got less enthusiastic.

One day, my dad had a doctor's appointment and couldn't call until later in the day. Let me tell you; the kids noticed. You better believe the kids were asking why "Doopta," the name the kids have for their grandfather, didn't call to sing with them. The kids are tied together by the idea of family and truly value the relationships, memories, and experiences that they share with their Doopta. So, the daily singing phone calls are now expected by the kids, and I know my dad won't ever let them down if he can help it.

Lessons from My Dad

Over my dad's career, when I was growing up, I saw him make a difference in the lives of others. He has traveled to Haiti countless times distributing shoes to people in need. Often, the shoes he has provided with his team have been the first pair of shoes they have ever had in their lives, or it's been the first decent pair of shoes they've owned in a long time. As a child, I remember him telling me about his different experiences and the impact that the people he came across made on his life. It was never about him. It was always about them and what the experiences and their words taught him about becoming a better person.

People often talk about my dad making a difference, but what they miss in his story is that he carries with him each person who has crossed his path. As much as people may be inspired or appreciative of who he is as a person, he's also shaped by the stories and experiences that he has with others both in our country and developing nations around the world. You'll read some of the stories of his experiences in this book, as he also conveyed in his earlier book, *Almost Isn't Good Enough*.

Shoes are something that many of us take for granted, but it's not possible for everyone to go out and buy a pair of properly fitted and comfortable shoes. My dad has seen children with shoes that are 2 or 3 sizes too small because their family has not been able to afford a new pair. As a mother, I know how that is not good for growing feet, and it's heartbreaking to realize that some mothers and fathers would do anything for their children, but the means they have are so limited.

I remember my dad expressing his appreciation for how hard people worked despite humble circumstances. He understood that because of systemic poverty, the deck was stacked against them. I also recall how he said that many of the families living in poverty never gave up and did not stop working until the job was complete. It's an ethic that we should all live by—hard work, dedication, a positive attitude and an optimistic and hopeful outlook on life.

Doopta in His Grandchildren

All in all, my dad's spirit is infused not only in me but also my children. Aubree is the most loving and caring little girl you'll ever meet. She worries about others before herself, and she lives to make others happy and smile just like her Doopta. Aiden is the child with the strongest will. He's a go-getter, and as my dad says, "CEO material." Aiden runs one hundred miles an hour and is also creative, like his grandfather. Jaxon is organized even at the age of one. He has to have things in line and in order, including when he gets his diaper changed—everything has to be organized. Jaxon always says "please" and "thank you" and is beyond loving, which are traits of my dad. As for myself, I put everyone before myself as well. I have always been this way, and my kids are my number one priority. My day is not complete unless they are happy and have smiles on their faces.

To say I'm my dad's number one fan would be an understatement. I am beyond proud of HIM and all he has accomplished both in his career and personally. He is the person I call if I need an honest opinion (even when it's tough to hear), a hug, a good laugh or even to get a high-five.

I hope after reading this book, that I have the privilege to co-author with my dad, that you'll discover something new, remember or figure out who you are tied to and how you can make a difference in the world today, tomorrow and in the future.

Melissa Elsey Pitts
Co-Author

CHAPTER 1
Pranāma

"Social entrepreneurs are not content just to give a fish or teach how to fish. They will not rest until they have revolutionized the fishing industry."
— *Bill Drayton*

Depending on your luck, life can change in an instant on any given day. I always tell my team to be positive and kind because there could be a "natural disaster" happening in the life of any person they speak to or meet but aren't privy to know. That's how my story as an entrepreneur began. It was as a distant observer of one of the most significant natural disasters in modern history.

Reverential Bowing

In India, there is a beautiful custom called pranāma, which means reverent bowing in Sanscrit. This bowing is done from a child to a parent or student to a teacher as a sign of respect and honor. Charanasparsha is a form of pranāma, and it is a bow that includes touching someone's feet. Again, this is a sign of deep respect toward elders or teachers.

I share this with you because some cultures, such as the Indian culture, believe that the feet are connected to the soul and are a part of the higher cosmic energy. Unlike our culture, where feet are considered dirty, for Indians and Hindus, feet are a symbol of deep respect and reverence for an elder. So, how we choose to look at things, our frame of reference, culture, and experiences color the lens through which we view the world.

A Shoe on a Beach

For readers who don't know my story, I'm going to share a little of it with you on these pages, and for those of you who know the history, bear with me because it provides the context for everything else in this book.

As most of us know, December 26, 2004, was a day that changed the lives of millions of people. In my home with my family for the holidays,

I was glued to the television news as the horror of the tragedy unfolded. If you're old enough to remember the images, it was utter devastation. As you know, an earthquake shook the depths of the ocean with a power of at least a 9.1 on the Richter Scale. This massive force under the sea caused tsunami waves that reached as high as 100 feet, which swallowed up everything in their path.

Those waves affected 14 countries, and as many as 280,000 people died in what is one of the worst natural disasters in history. I remember the scenes of complete devastation as helicopters and reporters showed miles and miles of flattened towns and villages.

And then came an image I will never forget. The news report on the television showed a single shoe that has washed ashore on the beach. That shoe, to me, represented a life. It haunted me.

The day I watched the shoe wash ashore on television in the comfort of my home with my family as we celebrated the Christmas holidays, I was the president of an international shoe manufacturing company. I had been in the shoe business since I was 15-years-old when I had my first job as a stock person in a shoe retail store during a work-study program.

I am not a Hindu, but to me, shoes and feet can be a masterpiece, art and indeed represent the miles walked by a human. Feet represent the history of a person concerning every place and experience they've ever had in life.

That single shoe remained in my thoughts.

In the coming days and weeks, I began to realize I had to do something. I couldn't live with myself if I didn't try to ease the suffering of the people who had survived the natural disaster in the Pacific. As a man in the shoe business, I understood the importance of shoes for walking and the prevention of illness. As I learned about the risk for disease because of so many deaths and decay as the clean-up began, I felt even more compelled to marshal forces to help.

Countless survivors had lost every material possession they owned, including homes, places of work, schools and everything inside of those buildings. Whole infrastructures were destroyed. If people had survived, all they had—barely—regarding material possessions were the clothes on their backs. Even worse than losing everything they materially owned, the loss of human life and the toll of suffering was extraordinary and too much to bear. The world mourned with those who had been affected. Something had to be done, and in my way, I knew I could honor the survivors by helping them get back on their feet and into shoes.

After the tsunami, inspired by that single news feature that showed the shoe washed ashore, I called on everyone I could think of and asked for donations of shoes to be shipped to affected countries. Candidly, I expected a few thousand pieces of footwear. Instead, like me, so many others had also been moved, and we ended up sending 250,000 shoes to people affected.

I remained as the president of the shoe manufacturing company, but my life had already profoundly changed. During the process of sending footwear to people in need in the countries affected by the tsunami in the Pacific, there was something inside that kept gnawing at me. As much as I tried to deny it or look away, I was coming face to face with the reality that I had to do more to help impact the lives of others. As much as a part of me, and many of my friends and family, would have been happier if I had stayed on the course I was on, a more significant part of me knew that I had to work to make the world a better place. Moving from being the president of an international shoe manufacturing company to shifting to something that would help improve the lives of others and make a social impact was only a matter of time.

Hurricane Katrina and an Earthquake in Haiti

In August of 2005, Hurricane Katrina originated in the Bahamas, and it became a destructive Category 5 hurricane. From Florida to Texas, once it hit the U.S., it caused incredible devastation and flooding because of levee breaks and storm surges. 1,833 people died in the hurricane and floods, and for the U.S. it marked one of the worst natural disasters our country has faced.

By the time Hurricane Katrina passed, I had already been working to ship shoes to people affected by natural disasters and families who happened to live in poverty. At the time, it was more akin to being a volunteer as I remained a senior level executive in the footwear industry. I had come to realize that being a senior executive in the footwear business allowed me to call on people to get help when disasters struck or ask for help for people in need.

Although my full-time job was as the president of an international company, I added to my load by creating a volunteer group called Katrina

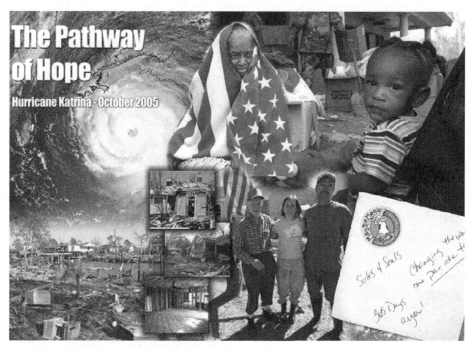

Shoes. I felt the pull to do both as long as I could, but it was becoming apparent to me that, ultimately, I would have to leave my job to become a social entrepreneur and follow my passion for social good.

As I wrestled with my path, and destiny, on January 12, 2010, a record earthquake killed over 200,000 people in Haiti and wrecked the lives of more than 300,000 survivors who were left with barely anything in a country that is the most impoverished nation in the entire Western Hemisphere. Again, I used my network to get to people who had so little the shoes they needed so they could get around from one place to another and attempt to reconstruct their lives.

By the time an earthquake leveled large swaths of Haiti, I had worked on transferring over 1 million pairs of shoes to people affected by

Katrina with the volunteer group, Katrina Shoes, and was now working to assist people affected in Haiti. The sheer logistics of consolidating and shipping shoes, not to mention collecting them in the first place, was becoming a significant effort that was stretching me and capturing more of my focus.

Ultimately, I came face to face with the reality of having to make a decision. I could continue to be the president of a shoe manufacturing company and live a very good lifestyle that included international travel, and which offered me a significant challenge in business. Or, I could shift my focus to humanitarian work shipping shoes to people affected by natural disasters and poverty creating micro-enterprise opportunities with shoes. I could not do both—or so I thought at the time.

You're Crazy…YOU MATTER

As I considered leaving my well-paying job to start a nonprofit out of nothing, my best friend and buddy, Fran J. Venincasa, told me I was crazy. At the time, I thought that if I wanted to make a social impact, creating a nonprofit organization was the best way to do it. In fact, I think most people felt that way since the idea of creating a for-profit social enterprise was not mainstream thought. I knew for-profit business people, I knew nonprofit people, but I hadn't yet met someone who had been a for-profit social entrepreneur.

I trusted Fran's insights because he was very successful in business and life. But, Fran wasn't the only one telling me I was crazy. Almost everyone thought I was nuts to walk away from an excellent executive position in a career I loved, making significant money in a way that challenged me.

At the time, Fran had been diagnosed with cancer. He was given a less than 10 percent chance of survival beyond a short time. It was with Fran that I had many in-depth and candid discussions about life.

Ultimately, it was two people that influenced my decision. The first was my high school teacher, Mrs. Busch, who provided me a lifeline—literally—when I was an awkward teenager who hadn't come into his own yet. After a devastating comment from another teacher who told me that in his opinion, I would never amount to anything, Jackie Busch sat me down and helped me believe in myself. She encouraged me and lit the fire inside that remains to this day, which is that every single life matters, including mine. It's been decades since she told me, "YOU Matter." And, those two words have been part of my motto for dealing with people ever since she said them to me.

The other person that helped crystalize my thinking was Fran. Although he was advising me not to leave the company, I also knew that Fran was focusing on the 10 percent chance that doctors told him he could overcome cancer instead of the 90 percent chance that cancer would end his life sooner than he or his family wanted. Fran was doing everything in his power to focus on that 10 percent chance of living beyond a few months (he lived another 10 years with that sharp focus on the 10 percent). He wasn't looking at the 90 percent chance he had of dying in less than a year. Fran was giving his life all he had. It was that focus that inspired me to stoke the fire for social good that was growing inside of me and becoming my passion so I could give it everything I had.

By the time I seriously considered leaving the shoe manufacturing

At one of the first shoe distributions to Katrina victims.

company I led, I had traveled and seen great wealth, as well as enormous poverty. I knew that developing Katrina's Shoes into something from a volunteer organization was going to be a whole new challenge and opportunity for me, and ultimately, it became something I couldn't pass up. Many people would continue to tell me I was crazy and the chances of setting up a successful nonprofit were slim to none since many charities operate with revenue of less than $100,000. But, Fran had inspired me to focus like a laser on the small chance for success of something I genuinely cared and was passionate about, which was to help others.

Be Crazy. Be Ridiculous. Be the Change.

In the intervening years since I started with that first phone call asking a shoe manufacturing CEO to please help me get shoes to survivors of the tsunami, so much has happened. I was the founder and became CEO of the nonprofit, Soles4Souls, which I will write about in the next chapter. That part of my life was then followed by what I'm doing now working to grow market share for my for-profit shoe drive fundraising social enterprises under Funds2Orgs Group.

The driving force behind it can be directly connected to the words Mrs. Busch said to me so many years ago in high school, "YOU Matter." Those words reverberated in my mind when I saw the single shoe washed on the shore of a beach in the Pacific after the tsunami. Each one of us matters. Each life is a gift, and every death is a loss.

If there's something inside of you that is also telling you to figure out a way to make money and a social impact, I'm proof that you can do it. And, I will share with you the mistakes and opportunities my team and I made as we perfected our work.

When I resigned as the president of a shoe manufacturing company to become the founder and CEO of the Soles4Souls nonprofit social enterprise, I thought that creating a tax-exempt organization was the proper way to make a difference, and so did the organization that provided us the start-up funding. Establishing a nonprofit was the traditional approach to social good.

As proud as I am of my time at Soles4Souls, I know that the for-profit social enterprise model I created with Funds2Orgs is better because it's a complete four-legged stool, which I will explain in Chapter 2. With time and because I gained an understanding of the regulatory and compliance burdens concerning nonprofits (rightly so, by the way, since they are tax-exempt), I also learned there are many ways people can make a difference in the lives of others and also create profitable opportunities, as well as help others raise money for their missions. Eventually, that knowledge led me to my for-profit social enterprise brands, starting with Funds2Orgs, which has now become Funds2Orgs Group with several shoe drive fundraising brands.

But let's not get ahead of ourselves. First, you have to have that desire and spark to be the change and make the world a better place. You have to prepare yourself to "be crazy," trust and follow your gut and take the risk to create your own business, social enterprise or nonprofit that brings light to what can sometimes be a very dark world.

To that end, not too long ago, I had a great conversation with my friend, Dan Pallotta. Dan's a global thought leader, TED Talk speaker, entrepreneur, and humanitarian. He offered me one of the best reminders about how to create something to reach an organization's highest potential. I loved what he said to me so much that I wanted to make sure to include it in this book so I can share it with you because Dan is right. If you're like me and those who work with me, who believe in doing something great and better than what existed yesterday, then Dan's words will hopefully bring you greater clarity. The ideas that Dan and I spoke about are encapsulated in a blog post he wrote,[4] which is one of the best motivational quotes I've ever read and am including it here:

> "Be ridiculous. If you're not being ridiculous, you're not exploring your organization's true potential. Everything in the world that makes us go 'Wow,' was born of some absurd human being with a ridiculous, impossible idea—from the Eiffel Tower to landing on the moon to the idea of America herself. We are taught that prudence is sophistication. The opposite is true. The most sophisticated things I've ever seen in my life—the most intelligent solutions to the greatest technical challenges in history—all came from someone being ridiculous. Ridiculous is what really tests us. Stretches us. Forces us to use the full measures of our intelligence, creativity, fortitude, and strength. Anything less and our true potential for intelligence, creativity, strength, and fortitude gets left on the table, never to see the light of day."

I've been in the shoe business since I was a 15-year-old kid. I have sold shoes, been the senior executive at several international shoe companies, founded a nonprofit which to this day provides shoes to people affected by poverty and natural disasters, and am currently the CEO of several shoe drive fundraising brands. If you had told me when I was a kid or even a guy in my twenties, that I'd achieve all of that—all with shoes—I'd probably have told you that it's impossible. But much like the reverential pranāma, or Dan's "be ridiculous," I found how I wanted to make a difference in the world, and I did it with shoes. You can too…dive in and be ridiculous!

---

4 "The Sydney Opera House: The Power of Ridiculous," Dan Pallotta, May 21, 2018, http://www.danpallotta.com/blog-1/2018/5/21/the-sydney-opera-house-the-power-of-ridiculous

CHAPTER 2
The Creation of Soles4Souls

"It doesn't matter how great your shoes are if you don't accomplish anything in them."
— *Martina Boone*

After the tsunami, I concluded that to make a difference I had a choice to make. I could continue to be a volunteer, as I had been while I led a global shoe company, or I could become the founder and CEO of a nonprofit social enterprise. The idea of becoming a for-profit social entrepreneur was not something that for whatever reason entered into my mind for more than a few moments at a time. I suppose it had to do with the fact that making money and a social impact seemed to be ideas, in practice, that were in different business realms. Most entities were either a for-profit business or a nonprofit entity (of which a not-for-profit social enterprise is an example), but few were for-profit social enterprises.

Although the modern concept of social enterprise goes back to the 1970s, the idea of social enterprises dates as far back as the middle of the 19th century with credit unions, as an example. I thought the better approach I had to take, particularly because there was a funder that was prepared to grant my team $20 million to get a nonprofit off the ground when I decided to leave the shoe manufacturing company, was to create a not-for-profit social enterprise. The condition of the financial grant was predicated on creating a nonprofit only. So, although I toyed with the idea of a for-profit social enterprise in my mind, a donation of $20 million to establish a nonprofit was a strong motivator to build a charity, which became Soles4Souls.

Years later, when I resigned from Soles4Souls, the desire to do something good had not been extinguished. I ultimately decided to build a for-profit social enterprise, Funds2Orgs, because it offered a chance to build a company and also make a social difference.

One of the key differentiators between Soles4Souls and

Funds2Orgs has been that a primary aspect of Funds2Orgs is to help non-profits, churches, schools, civic groups, and many others raise money for their organizations. Our shoe drive fundraising brands also help business-es demonstrate corporate social responsibility (CSR) leadership through employee engagement programs while raising funds for charities and good causes. The idea of creating fundraising solutions for organizations in our country and also helping to develop work and commerce opportu-nities for people living in poverty has been a thought that has intrigued my team and me. We firmly believe in creating opportunities through HOPE, and because of the people who work with me and our focus on this vision, we've made it a successful reality.

The Difference Between A Nonprofit and Social Enterprise

In case you think you'd like to make a social impact, I'm going to give you a quick lesson in the difference between a nonprofit and for-profit social en-terprise with the latter being much more flexible. A nonprofit is an organi-zation that does not have shareholders, and the not-for-profit, tax-exempt status is the tax designation given by the Internal Revenue Service (IRS). A nonprofit is held in the public trust exclusively to make a social impact, which is why it generally does not have to pay taxes.

There's a common misunderstanding that a "not-for-profit" can't make a profit or significantly grow its revenue base. The reality is, however, that it can make a profit. What it can't do is to disperse that profit to share-holders. Instead, what it has to do is to reinvest any "profit" it makes right back into the nonprofit entity.

A social enterprise can have more flexibility, depending on how it's structured. It can be a nonprofit. When it is a nonprofit social enter-prise, it has an element within it that is commerce driven. You've probably seen nonprofits that sell artisan crafts by the people they seek to serve. But, generally speaking, social enterprises are for-profits, and they are also businesses that make a social impact. In the for-profit model, social enter-prises,

1) Make a profit;
2) Pay taxes; and,
3) Make a social impact.

Why A For-Profit Social Enterprise?

I appreciate my for-profit social enterprises because my team and I have created winning situations for diverse groups—and made a profit. We've built a mechanism for a global social impact for people who partner with us across North America. We do this by partnering with organizations, groups, and individuals to raise money by collecting shoes. We issue a check to the people who do one of our shoe drive fundraisers. The thousands of shoes we receive from these fundraisers are consolidated and shipped by us to micro-entrepreneurs in developing nations. In turn, small business owners in countries around the world get shoe inventory to sell in their communities.

After I resigned from Soles4Souls, I realized that while the idea of micro-enterprise and helping people in poverty with a hand-up, as opposed to a handout, which began at Soles4Souls.

Soles4Souls is a nonprofit social enterprise that collects shoes and then sells the merchandise to micro-entrepreneurs in developing nations. That model has been very good for the organization, and I'm proud of what Soles4Souls has done, both during my tenure and also after I resigned from the organization.

I've always sought to build opportunities and, admittedly, have learned the hard way that nonprofit success can come at the cost of business flexibility and constraints.

When I started str@tegic, after I left Soles4Souls, my team and I were fully immersed in the nonprofit sector, and it was apparent to us that the vast majority of charities need to raise money in creative and engaging ways that go beyond the typical ask for monetary donations. Most nonprofits exist with limited resources, and many have operating budgets significantly below $1 million.

We were also aware of the demand for shoes in developing nations because vendors continued to call us, even after I left Soles4Souls, asking me how I could help them source much-needed footwear. My team and I also understood that if we repurposed shoes and kept them out of the trash, we extended the life of the footwear and helped the environment by lowering our carbon footprint. And, finally, having lived through the 2008 recession, which took many years for the middle class to overcome, creating job opportunities in the U.S. was also a priority in growing a business. I wanted to have the chance as an entrepreneur to provide Americans with job opportunities. Ultimately, all of those forces came together and propelled my team and me to build another business in addition to str@tegic, which was Funds2Orgs.

When we established Funds2Orgs, we created a way for nonprofits, schools, churches, civic groups, and others to raise much-needed money for their organizations or favorite causes by collecting gently worn, used and new shoes in shoe drive fundraisers. Funds2Orgs issues partners a check for the footwear; the more shoes they collect, the higher the amount of money received.

We work with hub operators and small business owners (also known as micro-entrepreneurs) in developing countries and sell the shoes to them. Ultimately, the footwear becomes inventory for people living with systemic poverty who create micro-enterprises or micro-businesses. The bonus is that shoe drive fundraisers provide organizations and their communities an opportunity to dispose of unwanted shoes in a socially responsible way and earn money. In other words, the for-profit social enterprise business model of a company like Funds2Orgs and the other shoe drive fundraising brands of Funds2Orgs Group is that it's like a four-legged stool.

The companies make an impact in four distinct ways. First, Funds2Orgs Group brands help organizations, groups, and people in North America to raise funds creatively without having people ask for money but instead asking communities to contribute shoes to shoe drive fundraisers. Secondly, shoe drive fundraisers provide inventory for micro-entrepreneurs to sell in developing nations. Work opportunities are limited because of systemic poverty in developing countries, and one of the best ways for people to earn an income is by selling merchandise. Third, shoe drive fundraisers make a social and environmental impact in that they prevent shoes from being thrown in the trash. In other words, it's a socially responsible fundraiser that extends the life of gently worn, used and new shoes. Finally, for the fourth leg of the stool, is that we've been able to hire a team of people (i.e., full-time, part-time, consultants and partners) around the world, but most are Americans, who have job opportunities. I am grateful for the fact that the Funds2Orgs Group brands provide jobs for people in our country.

Another essential aspect of our work is that micro-entrepreneurs who get the shoes collected in shoe drive fundraisers are not given a handout. In fact, in my conversations with micro-entrepreneurs around the world, I understand that they don't want charity. What they seek is an opportunity to help themselves. I've always believed that the best thing you can do for someone is to give them a hand-up, not just a handout. It's much more impactful than a handout. By providing people and families in developing nations with work and commerce opportunities, you offer respect and allow people the dignity to create their own businesses and solutions for themselves.

The reality is it would be incredibly audacious and arrogant of us to think that we could know what works and what doesn't for someone in another country. None of my team members or I live in countries such as Haiti, India or Guatemala. We don't have a deep understanding, other than the superficial experiences some of us have had when we've visited developing countries or had discussions with officials and community leaders, of what it's like to live in those countries. We only know what it's like to live in our own country. But, what my team and I learned and perfected with Funds2Orgs and the other shoe drive fundraising brands, is that we could partner with people in developing nations and assist them in providing opportunities. The rest was up to them.

$20.3 Million Kick-Off to Change the World

I did the "ridiculous" and left the shoe manufacturing company in 2006 and founded Soles4Souls with a group of other "crazy" believers who thought that we could create a better world and impact the lives of many for the better. The mission of the organization was two-fold, which was to aid people affected by natural disasters and also to support micro-entrepreneurs by providing them with inventory for their small businesses so that they can help themselves out of poverty.

Because of my extensive network in the shoe business over several decades, we received a grant of $20.3 million from the World Shoe Association to help get a nonprofit started. To have won an award of that size when we were beginning, demonstrated the belief that the association had in our talents and abilities to carefully manage the money, use it effectively and grow a nonprofit from my kitchen table to a respected global juggernaut. We weren't going to let them down. And, as the CEO, I also wasn't going to let down the small team of people who agreed to work with me, the members of the board and everyone who decided to support our efforts to change the world and improve the lives of people in need.

Within five years, we grew the organization from nothing to a nonprofit with an operating budget that exceeded $70 million. I've shared in my book *Almost Isn't Good Enough*[5] how we made that happen. This time, in this book I'm going to tell you the lessons I learned because the path to success is always through trial and error. Trying things out and failing might not seem like a fun thing to do, but it's the only way to be successful. The difference between those who succeed and those who don't is that those who make it happen, understand that they will have to continually test and experiment as they refine their work product.

When you're creating something new, and extraordinary, you're also going to have to accept the fact that not everyone is going to like or realize what you're doing. It doesn't matter. Your vision may not be something that everyone understands, but all you need is a committed few to make an idea a reality. Keep going. Do your thing and continue making your crazy or ridiculous dream happen, especially if you're creating jobs and opportunities for others.

Micro-Enterprise

At this point, I should write a little about micro-enterprise because it's been the basis of my work since my time at Soles4Souls. In the most straightforward definition, micro-enterprises are small businesses which have fewer than ten employees. As a matter of fact, by that definition, most companies in the U.S. can be considered micro-enterprises.

The modern-day idea of micro-enterprise is generally attributed to Muhammad Yunus who founded Grameen Bank in Bangladesh, which started the model of offering "micro-loans" to women, primarily, living in poverty so they could create businesses. The goal was to eradicate poverty by providing people with a chance to create their own business opportunity.

Yunus understood that there was a direct connection between poverty and business and work opportunities. If he was able to give women economic opportunities to work for themselves, the chances were high that they would be able to create sustaining incomes.

Yunus' model worked, and because of it, he earned a Nobel Prize in 1976. The model was brilliant because he was able to reverse that traditional practice of banks to have people provide collateral for loans. Instead, Grameen's business model with its clients has been one of "mutual trust, accountability, participation, and creativity."

---

5   "Almost Isn't Good Enough," Wayne Elsey, 2010, https://www.amazon.com/Almost-Isnt-Enough-Wayne-Elsey/dp/145074124X/ref=sr_1_1?ie=UTF8&qid=1530536966&sr=8-1&keywords=wayne+elsey

When people living in poverty apply for a loan through Grameen, they do not have to offer what they don't have (collateral) in exchange for the loan. With the obstacle of collateral out of the way, families living in poverty have been able to enter into the banking system, which when it was first done, it was considered a fundamentally radical and ridiculous idea.

Yunus' idea was smart, innovative and his vision worked. In 2017, 8.93 million people borrowed funds from Grameen Bank and of those, borrowers, 97 percent were women. The repayment rate on the loans is currently at an exceptional 95 percent with millions of people through the decades of operation having had the chance to create small business opportunities for themselves so they could escape the devastating clutches of poverty.

Generally speaking beyond Grameen Bank, the vast majority of businesses in developing nations are those with only one or two people working it. Grameen provides small investment loans, but as you'll understand more thoroughly in the next section, people living in poverty may find other ways to get the necessary resources to create a viable business.

Micro-enterprises add value to the local economies in several ways, such as creating work opportunities, building commerce within communities, enhancing the income of micro-entrepreneurs who often make more in their own business than by working for someone else, lowering the overall cost of business within communities and bringing an infusion of essential capital into a local economy.

A Hand-Up Versus a Handout
Specific to my work at Soles4Souls, the idea of micro-enterprise had been a seed in the back of my mind from the outset since I was aware of the model Yunus created years ago. In fact, I sent a board member of the organization to Honduras in the early days of Soles4Souls with 100 pairs of shoes. I was experimenting, which is essential for the growth and development of any organization, and I wanted to know if the shoes could be

sold quickly. Ninety percent of the footwear was sold within a week, which exceeded our expectations. It was a resounding success, so it was at this point that my team and I knew that a micro-enterprise model made sense, but getting the particulars of how it would work beyond those 100 shoes would take time.

Incredibly, when the board member returned, having sold the shoes quickly, he told me that I was crazy to consider any approach beyond disaster relief that would also include selling worn and used shoes to micro-entrepreneurs in developing nations.

He voiced concern about what people might say about selling donated shoes to people living in developing nations. He believed that people should be given charity, which is a noble thought, but we could also do more for others. He missed the idea of the social impact we were creating by providing micro-entrepreneurs with opportunities to help themselves out of poverty by creating commerce and sustainable jobs.

All I could tell him was that I respected his opinion, but in my gut, I knew we could ultimately do more beyond disaster-relief, and we could provide people living in poverty with something beyond a handout, which was a hand-up. I asked the board member to trust us, and soon Soles4Souls was able to prove that the burgeoning idea would work well with the sale of whole containers of shoes from North America to micro-entrepreneurs in developing nations.

Although my team and I hadn't fully developed the micro-enterprise aspect of the work, and it was more of a work in progress in the very beginning, we were still confident in the idea of helping to create employ-

ment opportunities for micro-entrepreneurs in developing countries from the start. We just had to figure out how to execute it well, and as is often the case, when you have big ideas, they take time to bake properly.

As Soles4Souls was developed, we made it a point to include in its initial regulatory documents, such as the Articles of Incorporation wording about micro-enterprise. As an example, the organizational bylaws stated, "To provide and to assist other organizations in the providing of shoes at little or no cost to individuals in the United States and throughout the world who are poor..."

These documents were also provided to the IRS as part of its initial application for tax exemption and were reviewed before the IRS granted us tax-exempt status. We didn't have it all buttoned down, but we understood enough that our work was always going to be two-fold: disaster relief and supporting micro-entrepreneurs in developing countries. We also realized that the micro-enterprise aspect of our work would take time to develop and would be created by trial, error, and the refinement of ideas.

Because I visited developing nations before I founded Soles4Souls, I witnessed first-hand the immense poverty that existed, and I understood that while aiding people affected by natural disasters was crucial, it was also essential to give a hand-up to families living in poverty. We just had to figure out how to make it a viable opportunity that made sense for the organization and the small business owners in developing countries.

My team and I understood from the beginning that we could help those affected by natural disasters, help families living in poverty to create or expand their small commercial businesses and make a positive contribution toward lowering our collective carbon footprint by repurposing shoes instead of allowing them to go into landfills.

The Soles4Souls team had so much confidence in our micro-enterprise work that even before we had worked out all of the kinks, we published a 14-page brochure in 2010 about micro-enterprise and Soles4Souls in partnership with Footwear Plus, which was part of mailings and tradeshows for Soles4Souls. In other words, we were moving at full throttle to help people affected by disasters and also to create business opportunities and support micro-entrepreneurs who had created small businesses in impoverished countries.

In 2009, I discussed the micro-enterprise model[6] in an article published in *The Tennessean*, which no longer appears on their website. The following year, I also expressed my views, which was the same year as the massive Haitian earthquake, in a *Footwear News* piece[7] where I was interviewed because I wanted the public to understand where my head was regarding what we could do to make a difference in the world. Haiti had suffered a catastrophic quake, and as the founder and CEO of Soles4Souls,

---

6 "Soles4Souls Microenterprise in Haiti," Republished, May 25, 2018, https://www.youtube.com/watch?v=Ldlg3Yiy1aQ&feature=youtu.be
7 "Helping Haiti," Neil Weilheimer, June 21, 2010, https://footwearnews.com/2010/business/news/helping-haiti-75783/

I went with members of my team as well as colleagues from the charity called Assist, which built orphanages and supplied medical equipment.

By the time the group landed in Haiti, we knew that it was imperative to create micro-enterprise opportunities for the hundreds of thousands of families living in poverty, and after the earthquake, in tent cities, because they had lost the little they had.

The reporter, Neil Weilheimer, wrote at the time after speaking to me, "He believes the quality of life can be dramatically improved in Haiti by distributing millions of shoes—a combination of new product collected from manufacturers and gently worn pairs donated by individuals—to help protect people's feet. The Soles4Souls chief also hopes to spark commerce by enabling locals with street-side shoe stores, or 'micro-businesses,' as he likes to call them."

As Weilheimer discovered by traveling with our group, I wanted to speak to and had the chance to discuss business with some of the micro-entrepreneurs who we saw selling shoes. Like any thoughtful entrepreneur, I had a lot of questions. Although the stores we visited were much more rudimentary than the ones we have in the U.S. (everything from sheds to blankets constituted a "store"), I wanted to understand the supply chain and how their business models worked. I took note of the fact that small business owners in Haiti were buying used shoes and selling them in their communities for up to $13 USD a pair.

What I understood by this point was that if there was a way to create commerce and work opportunities, people could begin to pull themselves out of poverty. It was one of those "ridiculous" ideas that took time to hatch fully, but my team and I knew it would be possible. Again, it was just a matter of thinking through the processes so that it made sense.

We understood that the creation of the supply chain was going to be expensive. Even if we collected the hundreds of thousands of shoes, and shipped them in shipping containers, we knew that the expense of each container would be a loss. We couldn't get the containers back to the U.S. filled with products because there was nothing that the Haitian economy was producing on a significant scale level that would make financial sense to ship to the U.S.

Although I had the brief idea of creating housing using those very same containers that were being used to send the thousands of shoes to Haiti for relief efforts, the plan did not work because of the heat within the containers. At the time, few architectural and construction companies understood how to adapt the containers and convert them to homes. A lot has changed since then, and containers have now successfully been modified to become homes, shops and even schools.

My experience in Haiti during that trip, however, re-affirmed what I had been working through in my mind long before our plane landed in Port-Au-Prince. By this point, Soles4Souls had developed like a rocket into one of the nation's fastest-growing nonprofits,[8] and we were looking to end our year with a budget of over $70 million. We had created the 1=1 model, and we knew that Haiti could be a place where we really could make a difference. If we could make a dent in this nation toward the elimination of poverty, we thought we could make Soles4Souls a $1 billion charity.

$1 Pair of Shoes or More

The 1=1 model is a straightforward concept that we developed at Soles-4Souls, once we understood that there was a need for used shoes in developing nations. However, to be candid, we've had our detractors on this idea. That said, it's a concept that is still used to this very day by the organization, and I suspect that the reason for that fact is that it makes business sense.

At the beginning of Soles4Souls, my team and I realized that we could provide each pair of shoes to micro-entrepreneurs for as little as $1. Meaning, with all of the costs of promotion for footwear, including billboards around the U.S. and the eventual logistics issues of getting the footwear to developing countries, the total cost for each pair of shoes was $1 to be sent overseas. As I've mentioned, since we were very excited about the chance that Soles4Souls had to help people out of poverty, even before the idea was "fully baked," I was talking about it publicly.

In the June 10, 2010 article that was mentioned above in *Footwear News*, I spoke about the idea of what would become the 1=1 model, "The Soles4Souls chief also hopes to spark commerce by enabling locals with street-side shoe stores, or 'micro-businesses,' as he likes to call them."

8 "Soles4Souls shoe charity takes steps to restore trust," USA TODAY, Bob Smietana, https://www.usatoday.com/story/news/nation/2013/03/23/shoe-charity-takes-steps-restore-trust/2013021/

one_one
dollar = PA)R

Anyone who knows me understands that my team and I like to dive into the deep end of the pool and begin experimenting with conceptual ideas. I've done this with groups past and present because it's a learning process. If you're looking to be an entrepreneur, this is an essential element on the path to success.

It wasn't long before we were talking about and promoting the 1=1 model to help people help themselves out of poverty. This model made sense because it works and has helped thousands of people create economic opportunities in the face of systemic poverty. I'm grateful and happy that the team at Soles4Souls believes in it so much that it continues to use it. I'm proud that the current executive team has maintained the formula.

Systemic Poverty

In the simplest terms, systemic poverty is devastating, and it's important to understand what it means in the lives of millions of people around the world who wake each morning trying to surmount the hurdles in the way of providing well for their families. By having an understanding of system-

ic poverty, you realize why micro-enterprise and the 1=1 model were essential for us to develop at Soles4Souls. We wanted to help not only the people who had survived natural disasters but also those who struggled to overcome the circumstances that made it exceedingly difficult to provide for their families.

Systemic poverty exists when the structural underpinnings are so fragile in a given community that they cannot meet the most basic functions necessary for a sustainable society. So, what does that mean? Let's take a look at Haiti as an example.

Haiti, with 10.4 million people, is the most impoverished nation in the Western Hemisphere and approximately 80 percent of the population[9] lives in poverty. According to the World Bank,[10] the following are a few of the facts about poverty in Haiti.

- More than 6 million Haitians live below the national poverty line, which is $2.41 per day.
- An additional 2.5 million live in extreme poverty, which is $1.23 per day.
- Economic growth is only 1 percent.

The realities on the ground can be heartbreaking, many of which I've seen first-hand. If you visit a developing nation or an area that has been harmed with incredible levels of poverty, you'll see and hear stories that, candidly, you wish you could change with the stroke of a magic wand. Of course, unfortunately, there is no magical solution to poverty.

Let me give you a lens into poverty as it relates to humans and shoes. In almost any place on the planet, to find jobs, which are few and far between in impoverished countries, you need shoes. At least twice I've fitted shoes on the feet of old men who could barely afford a pair of shoes; one of them was so poor that the day I put shoes on his feet was the first time he ever wore a pair. Think about that the next time you're putting on your shoes.

When my team and I have visited developing countries, we've learned about the local economy and jobs. Unfortunately, there aren't many jobs and those that exist typically end up going to people who are connected to whoever's in government at the time. The vast majority of people are forced to fend and figure it out for themselves. Some people will beg, and others will see if there is a way to create an economic opportunity for themselves.

That's where the selling of shoes comes into play with micro-entrepreneurs.

Countless people are trying to make a living, and they do it by selling products in their communities. If you were to walk through the main street in a city in a developing country like Haiti, you'd see a lot of people selling items that range from cell phone batteries to clothing, to shoes. Who's buying these products in an impoverished community? Other citizens living in poverty who need cheap merchandise. The need for products to sell is why it's vital, at least for the footwear business, to have

9 2019 Index of Economic Freedom, The Heritage Foundation, https://www.heritage.org/index/country/haiti
10 The World Bank in Haiti, https://www.worldbank.org/en/country/haiti/overview

a steady stream of inventory getting used and unwanted shoes to people who have created little businesses and work opportunities for themselves.

When a child attends school, shoes are a necessity and considered a part of a "uniform." Although you might wonder why this would be the case, it makes sense. Shoes should be worn for health reasons, which is something that many people in developed nations take for granted. Schools require shoes because they want the children not to get sick. The ground has parasites and disease-causing elements, which can enter into the bloodstream through cracks or cuts in the feet of people. Shoes protect the feet of children and adults from this risk, which can lead to illness, amputations and also death if left untreated.

When you have an understanding of what systemic poverty means, then you know how crucial it is to figure out innovative and "ridiculous" ways to provide opportunities to people living in systemic poverty to help themselves when their own society and government can't do it.

5 Years

Within five years, my team of "crazy and ridiculous" people and I created an incredible organization in Soles4Souls. By the time my tenure ended as CEO of Soles4Souls, I had demonstrated how the ridiculous and crazy idea could be done of providing people around the world, both overcoming the challenges of natural disasters and micro-entrepreneurs in poverty looking for a path to self-sufficiency.

I left the organization with gross receipts of $51.8 million, an inventory of footwear that amounted to $9.7 million and $5.3 million cash in the bank. But, the most significant legacy for me was that we had collected and distributed more than 19 million pairs of shoes to people who had lost everything in natural disasters and to micro-entrepreneurs who needed work opportunities. The fact that we changed and improved the lives of millions of people, some who we met, but countless people we didn't, is something for which I'm grateful to have experienced in my life.

CHAPTER 3
Experiences Had and Lessons Learned

"Failure should be our teacher, not our undertaker. Failure is delay, not defeat. It is a temporary detour, not a dead end. Failure is something we can avoid only by saying nothing, doing nothing, and being nothing."
— *Denis Waitley*

In the previous chapter, I mentioned that if I had to do it over again, I would have created a for-profit social enterprise. However, because $20.3 million is a great start-up grant, and it was a requirement of the funder, Soles4Souls was established as a nonprofit.

Little did I know that the experience would provide me with many lessons that ultimately informed and re-affirmed my thinking about how to continue to make a global impact with others once I left Soles4Souls who believe as I do, that we are all tied together and we have to make the world a better place.

If you too want to change the world, help the lives of others and make your ideas a reality, then I hope that my experiences will help you reflect on how you decide to move forward.

The reason I want to share these thoughts with you is that sometimes your heart can be in the right place, and your experiences could be appropriate for business. However, in practice, maybe because of regulatory or compliance rules or other reasons, you can end up with lots of headaches.

Although my team and I never did anything that would be considered inappropriate at a for-profit company, issues arose that were deemed not appropriate for the operation of a nonprofit. Each time this happened, we immediately addressed the matter. As time progressed, perhaps because of our enormous success, there was a group of people who wanted to take Soles4Souls down a few notches by creating and fanning flames, but fortunately, we were always able to rise above those challenges.

Fortunately, I understand that when you do something, often you'll get critics who feel a need to create adversity. Usually, it comes from people who can't do what you're doing. No matter what happens, never pay your critics any mind. If there's someone who provides constructive criticism that helps you improve, that's great, but if it's simply a matter criticizing for the sake of criticizing, ignore it and keep moving forward.

That said, let's break down each of the critiques that happened during my tenure at Soles4Souls so that you have the wisdom of our experience and how it was handled, as you consider your own plans and ideas.

CEO and Board Chair

One of the first things that became an issue of contention at Soles4Souls is that I served as both CEO and also the board chair for the nonprofit, which had been a unanimous decision of the board. Initially, it began as a whisper within the organization, but ultimately it developed into a situation that didn't serve us well.

I came from the for-profit sector, and it's common for a CEO to also serve as the board chair. Since the recession of 2008, this dual role has been reconsidered in many companies, even in some of the world's leading corporations, but when I set up Soles4Souls, it was pre-Great Recession time.

The fundamental reason[11] why the roles of CEO and board chair are combined in companies is that with a unified position, the one executive has the vantage point of seeing everything from the strategic board level, but also with the working understanding of the day-to-day operations as the chief executive officer. When this happens, information travels with ease since it's

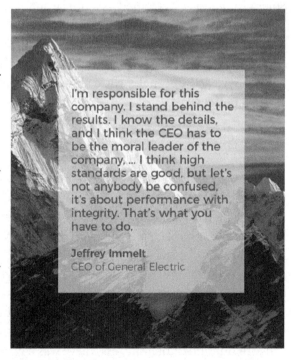

I'm responsible for this company. I stand behind the results. I know the details, and I think the CEO has to be the moral leader of the company, ... I think high standards are good, but let's not anybody be confused, it's about performance with integrity. That's what you have to do.

Jeffrey Immelt
CEO of General Electric

11   "Split Decisions: the Pros and Cons of Separating CEO and Chairman Roles," Corporate Compliance Insights, Michael Stockham, July 9, 2013, https://www.corporatecomplianceinsights.com/split-decisions-the-pros-and-cons-of-separating-ceo-and-chairman-roles/

filtered through one person who knows the board objectives, and also the managerial ones. That means that decisions are made more easily and efficiently, and most importantly, when there are issues that could become challenges, the CEO and chairperson can address these instances more rapidly because of their dual vantage point and roles.

When one person is fulfilling the role of both CEO and board chair, you also typically have someone who is strong, active and visionary, which helps to propel an organization forward. Sometimes, when you have the role divided, you might find the board chair who does not have the full confidence or trust of the executive team because they consider the chair not part of their group and not privy to everything they deal with on a day-to-day basis. In other words, separate roles can create a wall between the CEO and his or her executive team.

In the nonprofit sector, however, it is more common for the CEO not to serve as the board chair as well. The split in the positions is a reality in many organizations because nonprofits, being tax-exempt for the most part, serve in a unique place within society. Although we weren't aware of any laws that dictated that the board chair and CEO couldn't be the same person, as a matter of course, nonprofits tend to have different people hold each respective role. By doing so, it helps minimize any potential conflict of interest where a board member can do something that could be to his or her personal benefit, instead of the nonprofit's.

When a chairperson and CEO are one person, there could be a chance for a conflict of interest if you're not careful. Since the board usually hires and is responsible for oversight of the CEO's job performance, the biggest challenge is that a person in that role could keep a board from understanding problems or difficulties for a charity because he or she wants to preserve their job.

That said, just because you have a board chair and CEO as one person, it does not mean there will be a conflict or worse. In other words, this situation can be managed with trust, integrity, excellent communications and oversight by the board and the CEO/board chair.

I believe in clear and appropriate conflict of interest policies within charitable organizations, but there's no reason why CEOs and board chairs shouldn't be one and the same if the conditions are right. The benefits can be particularly significant when a nonprofit is looking to grow to scale, as we intended to do with Soles4Souls. The other situation that arose in my role as CEO and chair is the matter of salary. Yes, I had critics claim that I earned too much in salary as a nonprofit executive. I was not the first, nor will I be the last to face that criticism. It's an ongoing tension within the nonprofit sector, which is a shame because many nonprofit workers earn substantially less than they should be making for the work they do. At the time of the criticism, Soles4Souls had a budget that exceeded $50 million.

In the for-profit sector, it's acceptable to pay people a competitive salary based on performance. In the nonprofit world, there's almost a pathological insistence that its workers be underpaid, overworked and joyful about it. It's wrong, and that's why there's such a revolving door in the field. You have countless passionate people entering into organizations with great missions, and then you have boards, executives and even donors who believe that salary should be kept to a minimum. I think this is one of the reasons why we continue with some of society's most intractable problems. It's difficult to do great things when you have a revolving door with team members leaving nonprofits for better salaries.

As is appropriate, when the salary decisions were made for my role as the chief executive officer of Soles4Souls, it was always reviewed by the board of directors, without me in the room, even as board chair. At one point, the board hired the Center for Nonprofit Management in Nashville for a compensation study and followed their recommendations. Also, during that last year, I performed exceptionally well as the leader of the organization and had secured an $8 million unrestricted grant and doubled the outreach capacity of the organization. For a nonprofit with a budget larger than $50 million and where less than 5 percent was spent on administration, my salary was not excessive and was merely competitive.

My dual role as CEO and board chair and the matter of my salary were always done with full transparency at the board level. As I mentioned, when there were salary decisions concerning my role as CEO, I was never present, even though I was the chair of the board. In other words, the whole process was done with integrity and ethics.

Loan

In 2008, the world experienced the Great Recession, and if you were a working adult during that time, then you understand that the economic times were the worst since the Great Depression. On the day that Lehman Brothers went under, I remember how people thought the world was about to come to an end; it was that terrifying for society because we risked entering into another depression. No one wanted to go through a depression, and it seemed that we were on the brink. For days and weeks, no one knew what was going to happen, and it felt as if the country, and the world, had entered into a life-altering period. In fact, for millions of people, it was with difficult or devastating consequences as many lost their livelihoods, homes, and even their lives because of suicide.

Soon after Soles4Souls was founded, we set up a separate entity called Changing the World Foundation. The reason it was created was that we wanted to keep the fundraising focused and the foundation's sole responsibility was to do that, which allowed Soles4Souls to concentrate exclusively on programmatic work. I also had a nugget of thought in the back of my mind that perhaps someday Changing the World Foundation could also support innovative ideas and organizations looking to making a significant impact around the world.

In 2009, Changing the World Foundation provided me a loan so that I could refinance investment condos in Florida. Again, if you were aware of what was happening at that time, real estate rental property in Florida crashed. There was a housing bubble, and it exploded in a big way. The U.S. government provided $900 billion in loans and rescues to people affected by the housing crisis.

Simultaneously, we needed a way to guarantee Soles4Souls did not implode as the economic world got shredded to tatters, and there had to be a safe investment for a portion of its financial assets. In my business experience, as well as that of the business people on the Soles4Souls and Changing the World Foundation boards, was that executives of a business could be provided loans. It was a common practice in the for-profit sphere. (Later, the Sarbanes-Oxley Act changed the ability for executives to get loans[12] from their for-profit companies after the 2008 Recession). Therefore, we determined that it would make sense to provide me a loan, which would be safe since I would pay it back with interest as I was financially well-positioned despite the economic upheaval that was happening.

The loan was reviewed and approved by our legal and auditing teams, at the request of the boards of both Soles4Souls and Changing the

---

12 "Sarbanes-Oxley Act Hastily Extinguishes Executive Loans: Recommending Less Drastic Regulatory Alternatives," Suffolk Law Review, June 8, 2013, http://suffolklawreview.org/wp-content/uploads/2005/05/Sroka_Final.pdf

World Foundation. We wanted to ensure that the loan complied with federal and state laws.

Unfortunately, both boards and I were not well advised.

A year after the loan was made, the two boards and I were informed by a successive legal and auditing team that the loan violated the law in Tennessee and something like this was not permissible with nonprofits. None of us had any idea, and we relied on the expertise of the legal and finance professionals to guide and inform us appropriately.

The moment the boards and I were made aware that the loan was not permissible, I paid it back entirely, plus interest, immediately. Full stop. Once the new legal team informed me that the loan was not compliant, the decision as CEO and my recommendation to the full board as its chair was simple.

The legal team that had approved the loan had to go, and this was done expeditiously, and new lawyers were hired with full knowledge and approval by the two boards. A new accounting team that was well compensated was also engaged to make sure we never faced a similar situation again. We could never be in a position where the nonprofit laws were not understood by the people whose function it was to interpret them accurately. Additionally, it's important to note that despite what has been written publicly, Soles4Souls was never in any financial risk. I was financially whole, despite taking the refinancing loan from Changing the World Foundation. There was no way I would ever jeopardize the foundation or Soles4Souls because I was not ever going to do anything that would destroy something I so cared to see work and believed would help people.

The new legal and finance team made sure that the IRS tax filings, state filings, and all audited financial statements had appropriately reported the loan to ensure full compliance with regulators and the laws of the United States and also the State of Tennessee.

That said, during the period I thought that the loan was acceptable, I was operating with the highest levels of integrity, ethics, and concern for both Soles4Souls and Changing the World Foundation. One of the ways I accomplished this was that I negotiated a fixed and competitive return on the principle of the loan and collateralized it with assets that surpassed what was even required by the initial auditors who claimed the loan could be made without breaking any laws.

I wanted to operate from a position of respect and integrity to the organizations I was building. Ultimately, Changing the World was not only repaid the full amount, but it also made interest that was at a higher rate than what was available during this uncertain economic period.

Inflated Gifts-In-Kind

One of the final critiques against Soles4Souls, my team, and I was that we had exaggerated the numbers for gifts-in-kind to make the nonprofit appear more significant than it was. Gifts-in-kind are contributions of products or services given to a charity instead of money. Usually, these are offered by professionals or business who donate their expertise, products or services. The claim was that we were valuing gifts-in-kind much higher than the market rate. In other words, our critics were calling us irresponsible at best and thieves at worst. We were also criticized for categorizing any gifts-in-kind as revenue, which is acceptable according to generally accepted accounting principles (GAAP).

When the shoes were collected in the United States, the value of each new pair was measured at about one-third of the retail price, and the used ones were valued at pennies on the dollar, for accounting purposes. Remember, by the time that Soles4Souls received the footwear, the shoes were worn and used. Think of the concept similar to the depreciation of a car. The moment a vehicle is bought and leaves the dealership, it begins to lose value. Once a year has passed, a car loses between 15 and 20 percent of its value. The same goes for a shoe. Once it's worn, it's lost its original value. Our critics claimed that the reduced value we had placed on the shoes was too high, but they were not the ones who received the footwear, processed it and had their accounting teams evaluate their value. They simply were critics who were criticizing without all of the information we had in our possession.

The critiques have been hurtful, not so much for me because I can take it, but I've always been hurt because it was meant to question the integrity of an excellent and the talented team of professionals who were working with me at the time. That's unfortunate, but when you're successful, you will have your detractors. That's just a given.

My team always sought to do the best it could, and the in-kind numbers for the organization were *not* inflated. The in-kind revenue was based on the fair market value of the shoes we received, and according to the latest public financials for Soles4Souls, the way the inventory is valued is the same as it was since the start of 2006.

Remember, shoes that are used have also lost their value, but in developing countries, micro-entrepreneurs can make money on the footwear and the community can purchase items that they need.

Nevertheless, by the time I resigned my place as CEO of Soles-4Souls, I left the organization without any accounts receivables. Today, based on publicly accessible financials, it appears that the valuation for the shoes has remained the same as it was during my time as CEO.

Lessons Learned

I'm very proud of the work an excellent team of professionals and I did when we were building Soles4Souls. The group I had that worked with me at Soles4Souls and Changing the World Foundation were one of the most talented teams of people I've worked with up to that point, and I'm grateful we came together to some amazing things. I learned an immense amount from them, and it was because of their dedication to helping people in need around the world that we were able to create something very magical with Soles4Souls.

In this chapter, I've explained the critiques that Soles4Souls faced. I'm not entirely sure why anyone would want to question the work of any organization that is operating with integrity, ethics, and success in working to improve the lives of people in need. However, those critiques provided me with lessons. My subsequent work after Soles4Souls, I determined, that I was going to create a for-profit business that helped change the world someday.

With for-profit social enterprises, there's more flexibility, and there seems to be more public trust and expectations for social good by companies than at any other time in the past. As I mentioned, with for-profit companies, it is acceptable to have the CEO also be the chairman of the organization, but there are other benefits. For instance, it is much more acceptable to pay employees at a for-profit a competitive wage, and there is much less scrutiny[13] for doing so. There's more acceptance of "investing" in research and development; meaning, experimentation is viewed positively, and there is room to have higher overhead costs when there is a strategic reason.

Finally, one of the best reasons is that being ridiculous seems to be more accepted in the for-profit sector. For years, my team at Funds2Orgs Group has had conversations with people in the nonprofit sector who have their heart in the right place. Some of them have excellent vision, but little expertise or experience in the industry and they are learning as they go—with lots of pressure not to test ideas and strategies that might ultimately be great.

The grant Soles4Souls received helped in many ways, and one of the most significant was that we were able to obtain the expertise for

---

13 "Is A One Million Dollar Nonprofit CEO Salary As Bad As It Sounds?" Forbes, Investopia Contributor, January 23, 2013, https://www.forbes.com/sites/investopedia/2013/01/23/is-a-one-million-dollar-nonprofit-ceo-salary-as-bad-as-it-sounds/#3d55b36e42c7

running a charity from the outset. For instance, we recruited people with programmatic experience and had folks on our marketing team who knew how to position a nonprofit. Sure, we also had counsel that gave us the incorrect information concerning the loan, but sometimes these things happen even with the best of intentions.

One of the things that I wish all nonprofit leaders, funders, and the public understood more thoroughly is that the sector would have immensely more levels of success if the world viewed nonprofits with the same lens that they treat businesses.

When you innovate, you've got to be prepared for everyone telling you you're nuts.

Larry Ellison
CEO of Oracle

Think of nonprofits as businesses concerning most of their operations. Allow them the flexibility that for-profit companies have for the sole purpose of making a social impact. I bet that if we took the constraints off the nonprofit sector, many charities would be able to grow to scale and make even broader positive social changes in their community.

Alternately, the idea that profit and social good are not mutually exclusive ideas is something that benefits all of us. For-profit companies seeking to go beyond profit allows more innovative thinking for social good. It also permeates the thinking that goes through society with the thought that the well-being of everyone is essential. When you have businesses seeking to assist their local communities and the world in improving our circumstances, we all benefit from the thinking that we're in this—life—together, and it's imperative that we all help each other, even those we may never meet.

CHAPTER 4
The Reality of Lives Around the World

"Let us always meet each other with smile,
for the smile is the beginning of love."
— Mother Theresa

I don't want to minimize things in the United States, but compared to the rest of the world, we are wealthy—comparatively speaking. However, I do understand that in our country there is also a lot of poverty, which shouldn't be the case because of the immense wealth of our nation, but indeed, it is a reality. According to the Pew Research Center, in our country, 40.6 million people[14] in the United States lived in poverty in 2016. We can't possibly minimize the struggle that these millions of people face in our country every day.

In comparison to the rest of the world, others live in even deeper poverty. The Pew Research Center[15] reported how Americans lived in contrast to the rest of the world, and the results are striking.

- By global standards of living, 56 percent of Americans are high-income earners and live on more than $50 each day.

- An astonishing 32 percent of the U.S. population is defined as upper-middle income when compared with the global community.

- Additionally, 7 percent of Americans are middle income, followed by 3 percent in the low-income category and 2 percent of its population is defined as poor in comparison with the rest of the world.

- Globally, taking Americans out of the equation, 56 percent of the population is considered low income, 15 percent is poor.

14 "Americans deepest in poverty lost more ground in 2016," Pew Research Center, Kristen Bialik, October 6, 2017, http://www.pewresearch.org/fact-tank/2017/10/06/americans-deepest-in-poverty-lost-more-ground-in-2016/
15 "How Americans compare with the global middle class," Pew Research Center, Rakesh Kochhar, July 9, 2015, http://www.pewresearch.org/fact-tank/2015/07/09/how-americans-compare-with-the-global-middle-class/

Again, I don't want to minimize the pain and suffering of people living in poverty in our country. In a nation that is so wealthy and a global leader, there is no reason anyone should go to sleep hungry in our society, and each of us bears moral responsibility for our fellow brothers and sisters in our country.

However, I also think that we Americans sometimes fail to see the reality of the lives of people outside of our great nation. My hope in this section of the book is to inspire you to act somehow to help the men, women, and children of our country, or to look out to the broader world and see about being of assistance globally, in addition to any work that you might consider in the United States. Every one of us can help someone else, and it doesn't matter where we provide aid. We just have to believe we have that ability.

A Church Group's Mission Trips

The social enterprises under the umbrella of Funds2Orgs Group have had thousands of partners through the years, and one of our favorites is Hope and Healing for Colminy (HHC). It is an organization that was established in the first half of 2016. It was started by a woman called Glenda Powers, who is a former nurse, who became aware of the village of Colminy in Haiti. As you might know, Haiti is the most impoverished country in the entire Western Hemisphere, and it's a country where my team and I have been very involved in offering people a hand-up as opposed to merely a handout.

Glenda traveled with her church group to Colminy in 2013, and it was there where she met Rick Alford, who founded Destiny Village Orphanage. Glenda's church group had been supportive of the organization from the United States. During the mission trips that Glenda and other church members have done, they've distributed clean water, peanut butter bread, repurposed clothing, rice, and beans. As Glenda has aptly expressed, "These are simply temporary blessings."

It was after visiting Colminy for the opening of a clinic in the community that Glenda decided to create HHC because she understood the extreme daily challenges of the people who live in the village and she was inspired to do something about it.

The Village of Colminy

Even though Colminy's terrain is hot and dry, it is an agricultural community. As Glenda has described it to us, the "gardens" for the village are one to three miles away from where most people live in one or two room huts made of mud or concrete blocks. Within these humble homes, four to six people reside. As you can well imagine, the poverty is extreme, and by global standards, this means that families are living on not more than $2 a day.

In the village, there are no paved roads, electricity, cars or a sanitation system. What makes the circumstances more trying for women and children, in particular, is that they have to walk, each day, long distances of miles to carry back 40 lbs. containers of water for their family's daily

drinking, hygiene and sanitation needs. It is a very tough existence, to say the least, where, because of the harsh reality of life, Glenda has explained that the children are malnourished, with brittle hair and distended bellies.

Hope and Healing for Colminy

Having been a nurse, Glenda decided to target the community by providing as much as she could with HHC. With her medical background, she was able to research opportunities for delivering medicine and food. For instance, she discovered Med and Foods for Kids, which manufactures peanut butter and packages it in individual servings so children living in poverty can obtain necessary vitamins, minerals, and protein in their meals.

Glenda and her team raised money to staff a clinic in the community and named it Hope and Healing. The organization, mainly because of the medical backgrounds of several people in the group, have targeted treating children who are malnourished, but they also shifted their focus over time to create a water solution for Colminy. A village and its people can only thrive and overcome poverty if they can have clean water, sanitation, and hygiene.

HHC is committed to addressing water, sanitation, and hygiene in Haiti, one village at a time, beginning with helping Colminy become self-sustaining in five to seven years. They've started with water filter systems that are sold to families for 50 Haitian Gourdes, or the equivalent of approximately $0.78 USD. Glenda explained to us, "Experience has taught us that this gives owners dignity and pride of ownership. It also prevents the fight often seen with freebies. Recipients are also required to attend a class where they learn to assemble, use and maintain their systems."

HHC is but one of the stories of many from people who have decided to help others in need by giving them a hand-up in our nation and around the world.

Poverty Defined

Poverty has been with us since the beginning, but we know it doesn't have to be that way. While capitalism dictates that some people will have more than others, there's just no reason why we have to live in a world where people have so little that they go to bed hungry or can't afford to receive proper medical care. As I've mentioned in this book, there's a natural disaster happening in someone's life every moment of the day, and so many have been affected by the catastrophe that poverty can wreak on lives.

When I founded Soles4Souls, I believed—and still do—that what can make all the difference in the world is an opportunity. As humans, we live with hope, which is what propels us forward to try, and for most of us, the idea of opportunity is a base on which hope is founded. If we provided opportunities to others, more often than not, they will take the chance to pull themselves out of the space where they find themselves, which can be poverty. Unfortunately, the idea of opportunities is something that can be sorely lacking around the world for many.

Let's focus on what systemic poverty means for a moment so that there is more context around the realities for the people who are served by HHC, for instance, or the other folks that we partner with in developing countries with our suite of social enterprise brands.

Most people do not *want* to be poor. Sure, you may have people who live ascetic lives, such as monks or yogis and they deny "worldly" things to nurture their spirituality. They will deny themselves all worldly pleasures for a higher spiritual aim. Putting those individuals to the side, who choose to live an ascetic life, most people do not want to live a life that is impoverished or austere.

Most people want to have a job where they can earn a sustainable living wage for themselves and their families. They also want to know what it feels like to have done a good job and made their own way in the world. Contrary to what some people believe, poor people are not a group of lazy individuals who want to live off of someone else's dime. I never met a person living in poverty who could not feed themselves or, worse still, their child and they did not fret and worry about it. I never meet a parent who would not sacrifice everything they would ever have, including their own lives, to ensure the future success and well-being of their child.

However, there is something called systemic poverty, and it exists around the world in developing countries, where it is most pronounced, but also in our country. Unfortunately, millions of people live with a reality that is mired in systemic poverty, which exists because of societal and historical facts that prevent whole populations from having the *opportunities* that are afforded others.

In the simplest terms, you can think of poverty in two ways: 1) income poverty; and, 2), systemic poverty. Income poverty is very straightforward and is where a family's income is in relation to the federally established threshold within their country. Economists use income poverty to see how many people fall above, or below the federal income poverty level in each nation. If you fall below the national income poverty level in any given country, from the perspective of an economist, you are poor. However, social scientists take a more holistic approach to poverty, and they say that to understand poverty, you have to view the greater picture. This model addresses the concept of free choice (or as I call it, opportunity) to be able to control your future and success. In this second approach to poverty, social scientists look not only at income to determine poverty, but also measure other aspects such as access to quality health, housing, and education.

So, for instance, if you look at people living in a community such as Colminy, Haiti, where there is no sustainable water supply at this point, children and adults go hungry, there is limited to no education or job opportunities, the chances of anyone making it out of this existence are virtually impossible. Why? Because when people lack opportunity and are so impoverished, they often lack the skills, knowledge, access, and ability to be able to help themselves out of the situation. Poverty is not only economic. It is also historical, cultural, social and, yes, even political. In countries where there are ineffective laws, corruption or social conditions that benefit one group over another, an environment of bounty for some comes at the expense of opportunity (and poverty) for others.

According to UNESCO, human beings have the following human rights: "...economic (the right to work and have an adequate income), social (access to health care and education), political (freedom of thought, expression and association) and cultural (the right to maintain one's cultural identity and be involved in a community's cultural life)."[16] When that does not exist, people are living in poverty.

Lack of Opportunity

When I walked through the streets of developing nations in Central America or the Caribbean, where fundamental human rights do not structurally exist, I saw extreme poverty. But, as I mentioned, poverty also exists in  our country. For instance, I remember meeting a young man who was walking around with electrical tape holding the sole of his sneakers to the upper fabric of his athletic shoe. I remember asking the young man why he had tape around his sneakers. He told me that the sneakers were two sizes too small, and then he explained that he had the tape because his mom could not afford to buy him a new pair.

The young man was not yet old enough to work, and I know based on the area in our nation where he came from, he lived in a neighborhood

---

16   Social and Human Sciences, United Nations Educational, Scientific, and Cultural Organization (UNESCO), http://www.unesco.org/new/en/social-and-human-sciences/themes/international-migration/glossary/poverty/

where the educational opportunity to an excellent education was limited. I also knew that his community had a high level of unemployment and limited work opportunities. I wondered about the chances of him understanding how to get himself out of that situation unless he found someone who could help guide him if his mom wasn't able to provide the guidance.

If the reality of poverty exists in a country like the United States, which is one of the wealthiest nations in the world, imagine the life of people in places that have national political, societal, educational and commercial infrastructures that are mired in deprivation, such as a country like Haiti.

Silvia

One of my favorite people is Silvia, whom I've known for many years, and is one of the estimated 4,000 micro-entrepreneurs with whom we partner around the world. She lives in Haiti and is someone who has a bright spirit, despite the challenges that she's experienced and exemplifies many of the people I have gotten to know through the years in my trips to developing nations.

Silvia was living in extreme poverty earning less than $2 a day with her son, David, at the time that the devastating earthquake struck in 2010. As a single mother, she was doing everything in her power to survive. However, Silvia was full of determination to ensure that her son would not have to walk the same path that she had done. It meant that somehow, she had to provide for the education of her son, despite all of the odds she faced. She was determined, whatever the cost to her, that David remained focused on his studies and school work so he could have the best opportunities possible.

Silvia's dream was almost destroyed when the earthquake of January 12, 2010, struck Haiti with incredible force. It was a magnitude 7 quake, with a power that was so violent that less than two weeks later, the region experienced 52 aftershocks that were greater than a 4.5 magnitude. More than 150,000 people lost their lives and to make matters worse in such an impoverished country, 250,000 residences were obliterated or so damaged that people could no longer live inside of them.

Hundreds of thousands of people moved into a semi-permanent existence living in tent cities, which included Silvia and David. The repercussions of the earthquake reverberated for years after the earthquake despite the relief efforts of nations, NGO organizations and countless individuals who donated money, time, and supplies. In fact, I can tell you that the legacy of that earthquake remains today because it caused such incredible damage and destruction.

Silvia found herself with her son in the middle of this humanitarian disaster, and her dreams for herself and her son seemed to move far beyond her reach. Silvia's determination has always impressed me. Despite the setbacks, she would not be deterred, even in circumstances that were beyond tragic and stood monumentally large not only in her life but also in the fabric of her nation's psyche.

A couple of weeks after the earthquake a friend of Silvia's asked her to help her sell shoes in Port-au-Prince. People who have not experienced a natural disaster on the scale of the Indian Ocean tsunami of 2004 or the Haiti earthquake of 2010 may not realize that when the clean-up process begins, one of the most significant challenges becomes containing the spread of disease through contaminated water that runs through the streets. Often after a quake, pipes burst and water streams through towns, carrying disease. Add to that, people who have lost most, if not all, of their possessions including shoes, which protect feet from parasites and bacteria that can cause illness and lead to amputations and even death if not treated.

With her son as her inspiration, Silvia worked seven days a week and many times 12 hours a day selling shoes in her community. It took years, but she was eventually able to pull herself out of extreme poverty. She sold shoes in her town and with her warm spirit, courage, and positive outlook, she had many people who returned to her to purchase footwear. Through the years, while Silvia worked so that David could focus on his studies.

Before David graduated high school, Silvia had expanded her work and provided work opportunities for others who helped her sell shoes that are received from the United States in shoe drive fundraisers or through collection bins and then shipped to Haiti and other countries. As many micro-entrepreneurs we work with, when she became a business owner in her own right, she started purchasing shoes from Funds2Orgs for pennies on the dollar and then sold the footwear in her community for a profit.

Companies like Funds2Orgs Group, with its niche brands, want to make sure that people living in poverty have work, which comes by helping set up sustainable commercial opportunities. If people send donated shoes to developing nations as a gift, what can occur is that the market can become flooded, which drives people trying to make a living from selling shoes out of the market. When socially responsible companies or charities are looking to work in developing nations, it's vital to understand any economic implications and opportunities that may exist so as not to harm the people you are trying to help.

Today, Silvia has a thriving micro-enterprise business, and she earns more than $60 a day selling shoes in her community of Port-au-Prince. Additionally, her son, David, went on to college, which was an incredible opportunity—never having to cut short his education to go to work to help the family—and she was able to recruit other people in her community to work with her. In other words, Silvia was able to provide others with economic opportunities because of her own success.

David

David is another micro-entrepreneur who rose above the devastation that was wrought by the 2010 earthquake. One of the things I've always appreciated about the Haitian people is the fact that despite poverty, or natural disasters, their psyche is strong and courageous. Despite the heartbreaks and challenges that they face in their daily lives, they have a collective spirit that stands out. As a people, they have never been broken, no matter what has occurred in this small island nation.

If you were to go to Marché en Fer, the Iron Market, in Port-au-Prince, you might come across David. David works in this marketplace where the smells of Creole cooking and the energy of thousands of consumers and business converge. Every day of the week, you'll find a thriving market with people selling food, apparel, shoes, cell phones, and other merchandise. In fact, the reality for most people living in a developing nation such as Haiti, if they do not discover the path to sales, they will not likely not make enough money to live. Most small businesses in developing nations involve people selling merchandise to others in their community.

David has been one of the partners of Funds2Orgs for many years, and because of our work with him, he's operated a business, which has helped him improve his skills in math, reading and, of course, business. Like many people in developing nations know, being a "small business owner" can be a bit of a loose term. Often, people who are selling merchandise don't have a brick and mortar shop. Many times, people get started selling off a carpet or blanket where they lay out their products or on a table or in a small stall. If micro-entrepreneurs have a store, it may be more akin to a booth in a flea market in the U.S.

David began selling shoes on a carpet he would lay out on the floor of the market in Haiti. Micro-entrepreneurs that work with a company like Funds2Orgs Group have to purchase, for a small cost, the merchandise they sell. In other words, they have to make some investment in their business, which can frequently be somewhat overwhelming and scary when people have so little. But, it was with the support of his wife that David leaped to becoming a business owner. The alternative was living in extreme poverty, and with the shortage of jobs, the calculated risk of buying and selling shoes in Marché en Fer paid off for David. His first purchase was two dozen shoes that he purchased for a small fraction of their original price. He prepared the footwear for sale then spent the week being instructed by others on sales and how to run his business.

When he was ready, David went out to the market, laid out his thin mat and began to sell the shoes. His reflection on his experience was, "It was not easy at first, but I was able to sell all my shoes and have enough to help my family and buy more shoes to sell."

With persistence and drive, David grew his small business and, like Silvia, he helped others achieve success. David's wife joined him, as well as other members of his family and friends and with their help, he continues to purchase and sells hundreds of shoes annually.

These are but two of the stories that exist in countries like Haiti, where levels of extreme poverty are high, and work opportunities are low. It is changing, and world leaders have prioritized eradicating extreme poverty, but I can't help but think that in a world that is so rich with resources, it is not happening fast enough. Too many children die each day from not having anything to eat, which is a travesty. Too many parents and adults have to figure out economic paths for themselves with the odds stacked so high against them that you wonder how they don't give up.

Still countless people, despite the challenges that seem so extreme and monumental, get up every day and move the ball a little bit. Day after day, they rise early and fall to sleep late, moving things an inch at a time, and because of their persistence and commitment to better their circumstances, many do overcome.

We can each play a part in helping them do this, just like Glenda and many others. We can help pave the path for those who need support and help by providing a hand-up as opposed to handout. By supporting the efforts and lives of people in our local communities, and also around the world, one is continually reminded that we're all human and we're alike in many more ways than we are different.

CHAPTER 5
Everyday Heroes Giving the Hand-up

"Great things are done by a series of small things brought together."
— *Vincent Van Gogh*

Everyone can play a part, and everyone can make a difference and be a hero in the life of another human being. We just have to step up and realize that none of us walks this life path alone and it's always so much better when we're giving of ourselves.

Remember Dan Pallotta's words, "Be ridiculous." We each have the choice and the power to live our lives to the fullest, which often comes from helping others and being of service. We have the choice, to reach high and live an exceptional life experience in all of the moments of our lives, including the times we share with our families. As Dan said, "Everything in the world that makes us go 'Wow,' was born of some absurd human being with a ridiculous, impossible idea." It's vital to remember that dreams become a reality by just being aware, kind and generous of spirit to be a better person and do more.

The word hero comes to mind when I think of how each of us can become a hero to someone else, even our children. In my life, I remember when my daughter, Melissa, was a kid how she thought I was one of the coolest dads. Candidly, one of the reasons was because we broke the rules and what kid doesn't like a little naughty fun every once in a while?

One of my fondest memories is of the two of us test driving whatever bikes she wanted to try around Toys "R" Us stores as often as we could until managers informed us we had to stop. I know based on her thrilled exuberance and excitement after we left a store that she looked at me through eyes that admired me. I guess I was her hero then and I hope that I still am today.

I don't know about you, but in my life, I get a lot of inspiration from the lives of others, especially my family, but also the countless stories that I hear about one person doing something kind and considerate for another. The stories and the good things that are done from one person to another can be awe-inspiring, such as the stories of Silvia and her son, and also David, who live in one of the poorest nations on earth and still created a path for themselves and others to follow.

In this chapter, I want to talk about other everyday heroes. We all know about history's greatest heroes, but any one of us can be a hero to someone else. Most of us will not be the next Churchill or Oprah Winfrey, but, here's the scoop, we don't have to do enormous things as Churchill or Oprah to make a profound difference. A kind smile or word. A telephone call to someone who is alone. A donation or gift. There are so many little things or big ones that we can do to impact someone's life, and we never really know the difference we can make until we are remembered. How often have you done something helpful or kind for someone else, forgotten about it only to be reminded of it by that same person months, or even years, later? As Maya Angelou observed, people remember how you made them feel.

When you realize that YOU can make a difference at any moment, when you keep that thought with you throughout the day, your life begins to change. Those moments of compassion, kindness, and consideration for your fellow man, woman or child can happen countless times throughout the day. It doesn't take a lot of effort to be kind. It just takes awareness in a dinner to which you invite a friend whom you know is struggling financially, the contribution to the blood drive, or the candy you gave a small child who a moment before was crying because she was afraid.

Giving is a way of life, and it is when you understand that idea that you will see a whole new world open up to you. It's a belief, not only in your capacity to do something for others but also in yourself to be the best version of yourself possible—every moment of the day. It's not as easy to keep that mindset, especially in today's world of noise and increasing negativity, but it's possible. The world needs YOUR gifts. You have to believe that.

In this chapter, I want to tell you about everyday people who are seeking to change and impact those with whom they come into contact. What follows are vignettes about a person who was told that she would not live beyond a certain age, but she's still here and giving to others, a young pre-teen who saw another child in need and decided to do her part to help, and a business leader who has transformed what it means to wear red shoes.

First Volunteer

Many years ago, when I founded Soles4Souls, one of the people who supported my efforts to give people in developing nations a hand-up was Michele McDonald Owens. She lived near the street where the original warehouse stood where we would process and shoes we collected. Michele has generously been one of my supporters for many years, even today with Funds2Orgs Group.

Michele was the first volunteer at Soles4Souls because of her proximity to the warehouse. She would hear the trucks loaded with shoes making their way to the building, and she was always at the ready to lend a hand to sort and prepare shoes for shipment to developing countries.

Michele was born with hydrocephalus, which can be a condition that is acquired at birth or later in life. It is characterized by an accumulation of cerebrospinal fluid within the brain, which can increase pressure within the skull. In older people who have the condition, hydrocephalus can cause poor balance, headaches, seizures or double vision, among its symptoms. Doctors gave Michele a short life expectancy, just to 30—but she has defied the odds and today she is in her 50's, married with a family, and considered one of the longest living survivors with the condition. It has come at a price, including four surgeries, but she keeps focused on what's important to her and her life.

However, the condition has caused many in the business world to think her situation means she cannot contribute meaningfully, and that can't be further from the truth. As she has said, "Most of the time in the work world, I am just pushed aside because everything has to be done at such a fast pace." But, each of us has something to offer, if we only pause for a moment and see what gifts each of us can provide to the world. For Michele, she has a passion for ministry work. She has commented, "I was never expected to have, yet God saw fit to raise me up to show others that there is hope."

After a time of hearing the rumble of the trucks loaded with shoes heading to the warehouse, and because of her passion for making a difference in the world, she walked over to us and asked to help. Soon, every time she heard the trucks, she would promptly arrive at the loading docks to help unload the trucks and then check the shoes and ensure that they were all appropriately paired.

As she has told us, she saw a need, and she merely jumped in to help. That's it. Some mornings, the trucks wrapped around the building with shoes to unload, and there was Michele, working with our team unloading trucks. It was irrelevant for her, or us, that she has a condition that has caused, as she would say, "a lot of grief." She merely wanted to do her part to help us, and by extension the people she would never meet in developing countries, and we were happy to have her assistance.

There were days that Michele sat on the floor of the warehouse for hours surrounded by piles and piles of shoes to get them all sorted so they could be shipped overseas. This kind of work can be tedious and back-breaking, but Michele always did it with love and kindness pairing up shoes that could have easily been thrown into the trash had it not been for the people who gave them to us.

Other times, her husband and daughter who was being homeschooled at the time, would join her in walking over to the warehouse to help match shoes. In the wake of Hurricane Katrina, and then the flood in Nashville, Michele volunteered to do everything she could to make sure that we had the shoes properly sorted and paired together.

In preparation for including Michele's story in this book, she said, "I am a little bit from 'Old Hickory' with a calling in my life to do whatever I can find to put my hands in the work of the ministry. I will not give that up until I draw my last breath. I am pushing through. Whatever challenges come my way." People like Michele are an inspiration each day. She's a hero every day.

A Family's Love

I came to know of Tammy Bowers during my years at Soles4Souls. She became a passionate supporter of the work we were doing in the organization. She even co-authored an article about our work. However, Tammy comes to mind because of her unconditional love and commitment to her first-born child, Sarah. Tammy and her husband, Jeff, also have two boys, and like any good parent, they advocate for their children when needed.

When Sarah was 19 years old, she was diagnosed with a rare and incurable kidney disease that is called Loin Pain Hematuria Syndrome (LPHS). The condition is so rare that there are only 3,000 cases worldwide. LPHS consists of flank, or loin, pain, and unexplained blood in the urine. It is a debilitating disease with, typically, severe pain, sleep deprivation and complicated pain management, which taxes the organs and can cause other complications.

In her book, *A Journey of Hearts*, Tammy writes, "Life is about choices, discovering chances and making changes. If we only focus on the 'what ifs,' the negativities, wallowing in self-pity, we will miss opportunities that present themselves to us. I decided to take a deep breath, finding my inner strength along with some 'chutzpah,' to move forward to do whatever it took to help our baby. I thought the solution would be easy in finding a collaborative medical team, but in reality, it would be challenging, due to the rarity of her illness. I would keep the faith, not give up; I would find them, and their wiliness to give her 110% of their time, care, compassion, and expertise because only the best would do for our girl!"

In the years since my team and I established Funds2Orgs, we've had the opportunity to meet many parents such as Tammy who will do anything for their child. Like Tammy's family, they live keenly aware of the moments with some days being quiet and normal but always with the undercurrent that exists when there is a family member who has a serious disease. These families never quite know when they wake up in the morning or go to sleep at night what the next few hours or the following day can bring their way.

Living with a family member who is seriously ill is an incredible challenge, and while I am fortunate not to have had that experience in my life, I can only imagine how the senses of a parent are heightened because any moment could be incredibly profound and life-altering. Tammy's two sons have also shared in the experience, and she wrote that she has made it a point to support and encourage her sons in adequately dealing with their sister's disease. Admittedly, although at times they have not been able to know what to say or do, they've had their heart in the right place and understand that this is about supporting each other as a family because we're all tied together—whether it's family, friends or as strangers.

Still, Tammy and her family focus on staying present, taking care of themselves and doing what's necessary to support not only Sarah in her illness but also each other. Just like Silvia and David in Haiti, they rise above whatever obstacles life has placed in their way.

These people, as well as Michele, have a reserve of courage that runs deep. They serve to remind us that anyone can impact the life of someone else. It doesn't matter how much you have or don't have, or your circumstances—even in the face of illness; it's all about the human spirit, values, and priorities. Remember, at any moment, there is someone out there who needs our help. It could be a family member, friend, work colleague or stranger, and all we have to do is show up.

Red Shoes Living

We all have the power to rise. We can all help someone every day. That brings me to the unique story of Lonnie Mayne, who has integrated business and making a difference into a powerful message that has given hope to many who have had the chance to listen to him speak.

We know that business leaders can inspire social good and change. Sir Richard Branson is an excellent example of being a socially responsible corporate leader. Lonnie Mayne is another, and because he uses shoes as a representation of making a difference in the world, his company readily comes to mind.

Lonnie was the president of InMoment, which is considered one of the top customer experience optimization companies on the planet. Like me, Lonnie believes in relationship building and providing customers an exceptional experience. It was in that company that he created a team of "ridiculous" dreamers who thought they could change the world by recruiting "Red Shoes Leaders," who also believed in his idea of "Red Shoes Living." Because of the idea, InMoment grew by 817 percent because people are innately good, and when given the opportunity, most want to make a difference.

Today, he is the founder of Red Shoes Living, which he describes as a way of life. Perhaps you agree with Lonnie and me that negativity and destructive noise can be easily be found. You can wake up on any day, grab your phone and scroll through your social media platforms or the news and you'll likely see someone posting or tweeting negativity or ranting about an issue. While voicing one's opinion is good, there's just so much of it happening all day long in the modern era. I'm sure that you've probably seen or heard your friends say they are going to "take a break" from social media so they can focus on the positive. Maybe you've done it as well.

Lonnie and his Red Shoes Living movement is a voice trying to change the negative, which provides all of us with an excellent idea to support. Red shoes or sneakers are a symbol for Lonnie and people who have joined his campaign to make a positive impact in the world. Just like Dan Pallotta, Lonnie challenges all of us to get outside of our comfort zone and be ridiculous enough to think that we could make a difference. Lonnie believes in being bold, like wearing a pair of red shoes, to be the absolute best version of ourselves, and live lives that reach further than any of us thought was possible.

Lonnie spends his days challenging business leaders to create customer-centric organizations where the leaders are serving teams and the public within the company. He seeks to help business leaders around the world, including global brands, to develop high-performance cultures through authenticity and meaningful relationship building.

In my view, Lonnie has tapped into something that in business and life is something that, at the core, defines our humanity, and that's the need to be better and do better. Throughout history, humans have always strived to move themselves and the world forward through progress. It began when the early humans mastered fire, language for communication, art for storytelling, and eventually created democracy and civilized societies. More recent advances include landing on the moon and now moving toward Mars, as well as the development of modern innovations in technology and medicine.

We live in a world that continues to reach for places we have not yet explored both within ourselves and outside of ourselves. That curiosity and sense for adventure are why Lonnie has struck gold. He understands that part of being human, and he's going around to people to help them realize that although we have so much communication, the modern world can be overwhelming and challenging. Yet, the parts of us that drive inspiration, innovation, creativity, and positivity are all very much present and still a significant aspect of our human experience.

The red shoes Lonnie and people in his movement wear are a symbol of the possibilities for business leaders and for anyone who wants to live in a better world. Lonnie's message has gotten through, people around the world want to hear his words of motivation and also take bold action (represented by their wearing of red sneakers or shoes) to create positivity.

In one of his videos,[17] which explains a Red Shoes Living experience, Lonnie describes how we each have a choice to live a life of

17   "An Introduction to Red Shoes Living with Lonnie Mayne," February 11, 2017, https://www.youtube.com/watch?v=K4SQY_bnFm8&feature=youtu.be

mediocrity or a bold "red shoe" life. He reminds us about what it means to be the best and to live our values even though there is so much noise in the world today that we could easily forget. He inspires us to live by what is our true nature.

The red shoes are meant to serve as a reminder of the five pillars for Red Shoes Living. Red shoes demonstrate to others, and remind us, that each of us could dare to be different. The *Five Pillars of Red Shoes* help all of us live mindfully being the best version of ourselves in service to others and making the world a better place in whatever we do.

1. Awareness
2. Gratitude
3. Everyone has a story
4. Respect (Kindness)
5. Put yourself out there

If you've been seeking to re-affirm your commitment to yourself and the world around you in whatever you do, I have two suggestions for you. One is to get yourself a pair of red shoes or sneakers to remind yourself that you can be bold and different. You don't have to chime into the harmful noise. Instead, you can choose to live a life that's punctuated with bold moves for your life and that of others who experience your impact. The second thing that I suggest once you have those red shoes on your feet is to look up Lonnie and watch a few of his videos or read up on what he has to say about living a red shoe experience and life.

Never Too Young

Not too long ago, my team and I got to know compassion and kindness as demonstrated by Blakely Stawicki, who is not yet even a teenager. We got to know Blakely's big heart when she decided to do a kid-friendly shoe drive fundraiser through one of our brands. One day, Blakely overheard her step-father talking about a child named Michaela "Mickey" Merrill, who is afflicted with Sanfilippo Syndrome, also referred to as "Children's Alzheimer's," a terminal genetic disorder. Blakely's step-father was discussing a fundraiser for Mickey when Blakely over-heard.

Mickey's family describe her as a "bubbly, delightful little girl with a big belly laugh and a giant smile she shares with everyone." On the website for Mickey, her family describes the time when she was a baby with a period where she seemed happy and healthy. However, with time, and as the disease progressed, Mickey began to lag behind other baby's developmentally, which was most apparent in her speech. When doctors evaluated her, they discovered Mickey was nearsighted and had hearing loss. It was in testing to see if these two issues could be related where they discovered Sanfilippo, and she was diagnosed with subtype-A, which is the most common, but the most severe case.

Over time, a child such as Mickey who is afflicted with this disease loses their abilities to speak, comprehend, and to walk and eat. These are the reasons why Sanfilippo is described as Children's Alzheimer's. The average life expectancy of children with this disease is only between 10 to 20 years with the average lifespan being 15 years of age.

At present, there is no treatment or cure for the disease. However, research has been ongoing both in the U.S. and overseas, and Mickey's family, as well as the families of all children afflicted with the disease, hold hope for new treatments or a cure. Also, Mickey's family is working hard toward having Mickey admitted into a clinical trial, as fast as possible, since time is of the essence.

Although Blakley was just 11 years of age, she felt compelled to raise money toward Mickey's family's fundraising efforts to help her and for medical research through organizations such as Team Sanfilippo, which is dedicated to trying to find treatments and a cure for children like Mickey. Although I've never personally met Blakely's parents, I suspect that they never told her she couldn't raise money because she was just 11 years of age. To the contrary; I believe they supported their daughter's interest, especially because she was seeking to do something positive and good for someone else.

Blakely got on the internet and started to research how to go about raising money for Mickey. It was on the net that she discovered shoe drive fundraising and, as was reported in a Newark Post article,[18] Blakely said, "I wanted to help her. I found a kid-friendly way to help." With the support of her parents, Blakely started to collect gently worn, used and new shoes to raise money. The more shoes she gathered, the higher the amount of the check.

Blakely understood that she would need the assistance of her community in collecting shoes. She calculated that to get the 600 families she wanted to be involved, with most having approximately ten shoes to give, she would have to start big and that meant approaching her school with many student families. Blakely considered it and decided not only to assist

---

18 "11-year-old organizes donation drive to help girl with rare genetic disorder," Newark Post, Josh Shannon, March 5, 2018, https://www.newarkpostonline.com/news/year-old-organizes-donation-drive-to-help-girl-with-rare/article_db307c72-e014-5051-ada0-2b94b621eca6.html

Mickey but also to divide half of the proceeds from the fundraiser for her school, St. John the Beloved.

Again, at the time, Blakely was only 11, and she was a bit intimidated to go to the school principal to ask for permission to do a shoe drive fundraiser throughout the school. However, she was determined, and she prepared her notes for a small speech, which helped her gather her thoughts. When she presented it to her principal, the answer was obvious. Of course, she would be allowed to reach out to the school community for this special fundraiser.

Once she was ready, she was focused on succeeding in her fundraiser. She recruited ten of her friends to help her as volunteers, and then set out to collect as many shoes as possible, with their support and also her parents. Blakely promoted the shoe drive fundraiser by,

- Reaching out to the home and school association
- Sending mass emails.
- Placing announcements in the local church bulletin and community board
- Speaking to her basketball and athletic program directors to ask their support of the groups
- Posting on social media, particularly Facebook
- Placing collection boxes in the school for kids and their families to give shoes
- Canvassing the neighborhood and going door-to-door asking for shoes
- Using an app called Next Door, which helped them through social networking in amplifying the fundraiser to neighbors.

Blakely met her goal and gathered 1,800 pairs of shoes. More importantly, she was able to contribute to Mickey and also to her school. Blakely is another example that helps demonstrate that it doesn't matter who we are, how old we are, or what our abilities may be. All we have to do to make a difference in someone else's life is to get up and show up.

Think Kindness

In the next part of this book, Melissa will be sharing the awesome content that was sent to me from people who have crossed my path in life. However, there's one story that I wanted to place within my section of the book, which is about Brian Williams and his organization, Think Kindness. He's got the right idea, and I'm proud to know Brian and see what he's done with his organization, Think Kindness. Again, each of us can be the change and make the world a better place not only for ourselves but also for others. Each one of us can make a difference in someone's life and offer a path to kindness and hope. Brian's story exemplifies that thought, which is why I included it in this chapter.

The other reason I wanted to add Brian's words in this part of the book is that they brought back great memories, and candidly, made me smile. Here's what he had to say.

"To think that I've spoken to over one million students, documented over 2.5 million acts of kindness and have traveled to Africa 14 times…all sparked off a random phone call from Wayne.

I remember it vividly. It was a cold 42 degrees outside, and I was two deep into a three-mile run. The pace-setting music pumping through the headphones was disturbed by an unrecognized phone number. I debated whether or not to answer, but I was tired and used it as an excuse to take a break and let my heart settle.

'Hello?' I answered.

'Hi, Brian. My name is Wayne Elsey. I'm the founder of Soles4Souls,' said Wayne in a boisterous voice.

I could tell he was on a speakerphone.

At this time, I was trying to figure out how I could pursue a career in becoming a motivational speaker. My goal was to inspire students across the country to incorporate giving and kindness into their daily lives and future careers. I just wrapped up a massive kindness tour in my home-town of Reno, NV. But rather than just talk about small everyday acts of kindness that could take place in the halls of the schools, we wanted to go bigger. We set a goal to collect 5,000 pairs for needy children. But to make it even more difficult, we wanted to do it in just 15 days! Yes, it was ambitious. Even the local media doubted the success and used language such as, 'Local students *think* they can collect 5,000 shoes.'

Well, we didn't collect 5,000.

We collected 8,000.

Now I needed to figure out how to get them out of my garage and to the areas in need. A small logistic challenge I happened to look over when we started.

Back to the conversation.

'Hi, how are you?' I quickly replied.

'Doing good. Hey, I'm not interrupting you, am I?' he asked politely.

'No. Not at all,' I said standing on the side of a windy road in the high sierra mountains where every breath I took was visible.

'So, I heard about your shoe drive,' Wayne said and continued, 'I wanted to let you know that we can 100% take care of the shoes. But I wanted to talk to you about your school program and ways we may be able to collaborate. I'd like to fly you down to Nashville to meet my team and toss around some ideas.'

'Yes, would love to!' I answered back.

'Okay, how does next Tuesday work?' he responded.

It was less than a week away.

'Tuesday works perfectly,' I said without even considering if I would be given the time off at work.

'Okay, I'll have my assistant reach out with your flight and hotel details,' Wayne said.

Five days later I was on a plane to Nashville and meeting the founder of the largest shoe charity in the United States. Of course, I was nervous, but upon meeting him was taken aback by how relatable he was. Here I was meeting a guy that left a successful corporate career to start a nonprofit anchored in kindness.

One thing about Wayne is that he is genuine and is 100% present. If he talks to you—he talks to you and gives his whole undivided attention. Here I was meeting a CEO that runs a multi-million-dollar charity with hundreds of emails, contacts and phone calls each day—he didn't let one of them through. He gave me his undivided attention for nearly the entire day.

At this point my career I've spoken to maybe 15 schools as a 'motivational speaker.' Of those, none of them were a paid engagement. As I said, I was *pursuing* a career in motivational speaking, but at this time, it was more of a hobby than a career.

We were sitting in a large conference room. Photos of children receiving shoes in developing countries lined the walls. Wayne was sitting right next to me with other team members around the table.

'I like to find talented people and give them the resources they need to succeed,' said Wayne. 'How can I help you inspire more schools?' he added.

'To be honest. Money. Right now, I'm not getting paid; if I was paid, I could quit my job and go at it 100%,' I said frankly.

'Okay. Done. Now let's talk how we are going to grow this across the country,' he said.

In a matter of weeks, I quit my job and moved to Nashville. Over the next 12 months, we spoke to over 65 schools from coast-to-coast, documented over 250,000 acts of kindness and collected semi-trucks full of shoes.

This was the launching pad of Think Kindness, a nonprofit I founded in 2009 dedicated to inspiring kindness in schools across the country. To date, we've spoken to over 750 schools, documented over 2.5 million acts of kindness and watched entire school communities transform. We've mastered the art of 'Making Kindness Cool' and are now sparking waves of kindness from coast to coast.

Every act of kindness, no matter how small, truly matters. If a picture is worth a thousand words, then an act of kindness is worth a thousand pictures."

– Brian Williams, President & Founder, Think Kindness

If you would like to see Brian's work in action, you can watch his documentary *INSPIRE HOPE* on Amazon, which follows the impact a small act of kindness has on children around the world. Brian is another person who demonstrates that we can all be "ridiculous" with an idea to do something global for others, which will make a positive difference.

I'm sure that Brian must have had detractors or people who thought the idea to document millions of acts of kindness was ridiculous and crazy in the beginning. Perhaps they also told him that an organization set around that idea was not workable. But, I know Brian, and I think he understood that the world needs do-gooders and that the most significant ideas can be the craziest, but the most fun and impactful. I know that Brian realized that it's doable, and all he had to do was...do it.

Show Up

These are just a few of my favorite stories about getting out there and helping in whatever way, but there are countless stories about people who have stepped up to help someone else.

Perhaps you know of stories about a young child similar to Blakely, seasoned professionals like Lonnie and Brian, or a person who faces great odds and then steps up to volunteer like Michele. We all can make someone's burden less. We just have to choose to do it in whatever way we can.

CHAPTER 6
There is No Plan B

"Simply show up. Just put your soul into it. If you show up physically with the soles of your feet, the heart, mind, and soul will have a chance to follow or catch up. You may not want to be there in the beginning, but showing up allows a committed chance at making a difference every day for the people you love, the people you will meet, and the eventual person you will become. Show up."
— *Holli Gran*

I've promised that I would speak about how you could make a difference, and we're almost there. In fact, I have a more substantial offer for you. I'm going to invite you to join a movement of "ridiculous" people who believe that they can change the world, by joining us or by striking out on your own in your social enterprise.

However, before we get there, which will begin in the next chapter, I want to speak a little about our planet. The vast majority of people are concerned about climate change and what is happening with the increases in the intensity of storms, such as hurricanes or heat waves. To add to the stresses on the resources of our planet, we will have 11 billion people living in the world by the close of the 21st Century. Scientists are concerned, and so are people who understand that we have no viable option for a second planet at the moment. Maybe we will someday, but we don't have it now.

Therefore, each one of us has an obligation not only to ourselves and our families but also to our neighbors and people around the world whom we will never meet. We have to try in some way to make life on this planet more sustainable. We have to address climate change. We have to figure out innovative ways to ensure there are enough resources for the billions of people who live on this planet, including clean and potable water, sufficient and nutritious food, essential healthcare, and economic opportunities. Every working age adult should know of the pride of work and the ability to provide well for his or her family because of it.

That said, although every single one of us can and should make a difference, to be successful, we have to focus where we think we can do it. If you want to be successful, you can't have a scattershot approach. It doesn't work. I've decided to continue my decade's long career in the shoe business by continuing to grow and develop the various shoe drive fundraising brands in Funds2Orgs Group.

My team and I are also reaching beyond that suite of brands, and as I write this book, we're launching Head2Toe Recycling. The company works with retailers, corporations and individuals to provide them with a proven recycling program for clothing and shoes. In the following chapters, you'll have a chance to have a birds-eye view of a case study of why my team and I have started a recycling company, which you can use as a model for starting your own business, should you choose.

The Waste We Make

I care very much about climate change because of my time in the footwear business has shown me how much we waste. One of the dirty little secrets that the top shoe brands don't want you to know is that they destroy, often by burning, millions of shoes each year that were not sold because they want to maintain their brand status and don't want the shoes to go into a secondary market that could tarnish their brand.

While I understand the need to protect a brands image, I've felt uncomfortable about the destruction of shoes, especially in a way that adds to our climate challenges. Secondly, since I've spent time in developing nations and speaking with people who could use footwear, clothing and other merchandise to help them create sustainable incomes, I also think that the destruction of shoes by brands is a missed opportunity.

Allow me a few minutes to paint you a picture about what it means to throw clothing and shoes and other textiles into the trash before I provide you with insights on how to have all of us be better and more socially responsible. Let's begin with reporting by the Environmental Protection Agency[19] from 2015, which is the latest information available as of the writing of this book.

- Approximately 262 million tons of municipal solid waste (MSW) were generated.
- 68 million tons of MSW were recycled.

19 "Advancing Sustainable Materials Management: 2015 Fact Sheet: Assessing Trends in Material Generation, Recycling, Composting, Combustion with Energy Recovery and Landfilling in the United States," Environmental Protection Agency, July 2018, https://www.epa.gov/sites/production/files/2018-07/documents/2015_smm_msw_factsheet_07242018_fnl_508_002.pdf

- 23 million tons of MSW were composted.
- The 91 million tons of municipal solid waste that have been recycled or composted, represents 34.7 percent of the total MSW.
- Textiles, including clothing and shoes, represent 16.03 million tons and 65.7 percent of landfills.
- On a daily basis, every American produces 4.48 pounds of waste.
- Clothing is generally assumed to be in use by people in our country for fewer than 3 years.

Did you know that 99 percent of textiles are recyclable? Think about that number for a moment. What a tragedy and how wasteful that many in our society don't realize that they hurt the environment by not tossing old clothes or shoes into the garbage. The vast majority of the world's population, 70 percent,[20] uses

second-hand clothing, and they can use the millions of clothes and shoes that are simply thrown away in the garbage.

Specific to the recycling of clothing and shoes, Americans can be wasteful. Many of us live a life of excess because often we can view "success" through the bigger home, car, toys, and closets full of stuff, which is why books and shows about downsizing and being a minimalist are so popular. All of this ultimately creates waste and, candidly garbage, when we no longer want to wear last year's clothing, footwear or want to continue to use the items we own. Here's the reality of the situation: the public—you and I included—are the most significant contributors to landfills. Corporations or other groups are not the most significant segments which fill up landfills. It's us.

In fact, as was reported by Southern Indiana University, "The U.S. is the #1 trash-producing country in the world at 1,609 pounds per person per year. This means that 5% of the world's people generate 40% of the world's waste."[21]

Around the country, some communities have textile recycling pro-

20 "Textile Recycling Facts and Figures," The Balance, Small Business, Rick Leblanc, September 24, 2018, https://www.thebalancesmb.com/textile-recycling-facts-and-figures-2878122
21 "Solid Waste & Landfill Facts," University of Southern Indiana, https://www.usi.edu/recycle/solid-waste-landfill-facts

grams, but 85 percent of waste still goes to landfills. The U.S. needs landfill space, especially now that China is no longer accepting[22] certain types of our waste. Our country exports about a third of our total waste abroad, and China has decided to ban 24 types of solid waste it will no longer accept, and it's causing problems for municipalities in the U.S.

Let's take this one step further and go beyond garbage dumps. When we throw our clothing and shoes into the trash, we're not only adding waste to landfills; we're also wasting other resources. For instance, it's not merely those textiles, but we're spending the water and all of the energy that went into manufacturing those articles. When we choose not to repurpose or recycle, we're growing landfills, wasting water, electricity, and energy in the creation of the items. Taking the time to reuse and repurpose clothing and shoes outweigh any inconvenience of doing so. There are ways you can choose never to throw away a piece of clothing or a pair of shoes again, and one of them is by looking for companies that will recycle or repurpose the merchandise.

The Benefits of Recycling and Repurposing

I'm going to share with you another fact that you might not know. 90 to 95 percent of textiles can be recycled or repurposed. In other words, if each of us looked at the clothing, shoes, linens, curtains, carpets, and other textiles in our homes that we're thinking about getting rid of in the trash because we want something new, someone else in a developing nation can use 90 percent of those items.

By taking just a little bit of time to discover companies or organizations that are responsible social enterprises in the recycling or repurposing industry, you can set yourself on the path to helping our planet, and micro-entrepreneurs in developing nations who are just looking for a sustainable economic opportunity to work. Remember the stories of Silvia

---

22   "Recycling Chaos In U.S. As China Bans 'Foreign Waste,'" NPR, Morning Edition, https://www.npr.org/2017/12/09/568797388/recycling-chaos-in-u-s-as-china-bans-foreign-waste

and David. There are thousands of others, millions, like them.

When you're thinking of what you dispose of and how it allows you to make a significant contribution to the sustainability of our planet; you can also improve the lives of thousands of people around the world.

More than 70 percent of the global population[23] uses second-hand clothing and shoes. Not only can people use the clothing and shoes as second-hand items, but the materials of these items can also be repurposed for cleaning supplies, insulation, upholstery or even mattresses.

Before I get into the critical benefits of recycling and repurposing, I think it might be a good idea to define what each of them means for more clarity. The easiest way to do it, because it's convenient and straightforward to understand, is by telling you briefly about the difference between Funds2Orgs Group and Head2Toe Recycling.

Funds2Orgs Group never uses the word recycling because we don't do it. It's a fundraising company first and foremost and issues a check for the shoes it receives to its fundraising partners. The company repurposes the shoes we receive. So, if you take a look at our marketing material, you'll always see the words "gently worn, used and new shoes." There's a reason for this. What we're doing is making sure that people who are collecting or contributing to a shoe drive fundraiser understand that we have to have the shoes in as new a condition as possible. Repurposing necessitates retaining as much of the original state of the shoe as possible.

Recycling is different, and for my team and I, this is where Head-2Toe Recycling comes into the picture. When you recycle something, you're looking to reuse an item, not throw it into the trash and use it in another way. So, in our example, this could mean taking the shoes that do not have pairs and hence can't be used by a person, to be torn apart for their material. For instance, the rubber can be used to create something new, like playgrounds. Clothing that is no sellable can be cut and turned into cleaning rags.

The distinction may be subtle to those who are not in the business, but it's essential. With that understanding, we can move forward into the different benefits of recycling or repurposing.

Reduction of landfill space

When you recycle the clothing or shoes that you don't want, you're helping the environment. You might not know, but synthetics do not decompose (so minimize those purchases). Synthetic fiber products will not decay,

23   "Textile Recycling Facts and Figures," The Balance, Small Business, Rick Leblanc, September 24, 2018, https://www.thebalancesmb.com/textile-recycling-facts-and-figures-2878122

and as a result, present a unique set of problems in the landfill. Wool decomposes, but as it does, it produces harmful methane, which contributes to global climate change and harms the health of people who live near open landfills.

Recycling unwanted clothing reduces landfill waste as well as the number of resources needed to create new clothing. It also lessens the energy and waste produced by the manufacturing process—clothing scraps from making clothes end up in landfills. Instead, used clothing can be donated, sold or disassembled for the fabric.

Development of Additional Markets

When you allow your clothing and shoes to be shipped to people in developing countries, you're helping to create markets in their communities. Not only can apparel business owners sell the second-hand clothing and shoes, but you have other markets that open up.

As an example, Funds2Orgs Group sends any single shoes that we receive in error in our shoe drive fundraisers and any excess scraps to Pakistan where these items are consolidated and processed in volume. The material is used to create new products, such as mattresses or upholstery. An added benefit is that products used with recycled materials generally cost less to produce, which is a crucial benefit for both micro-businesses and consumers in developing nations.

Conservation

When each of us takes the time to find ways to recycle and repurpose our clothing and footwear, we're doing our part in helping conserve. As I alluded to earlier, it takes other natural resources and power to create textiles from their original materials. There is electricity and water, for instance, that are needed to develop new apparel.

When textiles are given to others in developing nations, we're helping conserve necessary energy and resources. Instead of having factories burn through even more of these resources to create clothing and footwear for the nearly 8 billion people who currently live on this planet, which harms the environment, recycling conserves.

Paris Climate Agreement

There has been a lot of discussion about the decision by President Donald Trump to pull the United States out of the Paris Climate Agreement. However, the U.S. is still doing its part. Despite the federal government withdrawing, state governors have formed the United States Climate Alliance.

Seventeen governors have pledged, in a bipartisan sign of unity, to do their part to meet the goals of the Paris Climate Accord.

Also, over 400 Republican and Democratic mayors across our great nation have also joined together in a coalition called Climate Mayors. They too are looking to continue to work together to minimize climate change and exchange initiatives and ideas for meaningful efforts in their local communities. Climate Mayors represent more than 70 million Americans. What this means is that cities across America are looking for ways to be socially responsible concerning climate change, and this is an excellent opportunity for those of us who want to impact the world positively.

Environmental Benefits

The environmental benefits of repurposing and recycling are massive. There are several key benefits of recycling clothing and shoes in particular. As an example, there is a reduction in the pesticides used to grow the cotton or the making of fabrics from petroleum sources and the water needed to dye textile fabrics.

Other pluses include that the pollutants that are emitted, are lessened when people recycle and repurpose. The reduction lowers the greenhouse gases and volatile and harmful organic compounds that are released both into the air and also the water from the manufacturing process.

Commerce

People living in developing nations, millions who live in poverty, need economic opportunities. There is a desperate need for sustainable jobs and work opportunities. Families living in conditions of systemic poverty have to help themselves because the usual societal structures that might be able to lend a hand, such as government, businesses, or NGOs, don't have the infrastructure or ability to be of assistance.

When people recycle or repurpose their clothing, it provides people in developing countries with a viable path out of poverty, which they must create for themselves. As I've written, businesses like Funds2Orgs Group or Head2Toe Recycling sell the shoes or clothing to small business owners for low prices. The micro-entrepreneurs then clean up the products and get them ready to sell in their local markets for a profit.

Remember, also what I described earlier in this book. The reason we sell the shoes and clothing and do not give it away is that if we did so, we would be harming the very people we are trying to assist with commercial opportunities. Flooding the market with free clothing and shoes destroys jobs. Local governments understand this, and some have created laws making it illegal to give away merchandise.

Consumer and Industry Benefits

When consumers around the world purchase recycled clothing or footwear, the pricing is lower, and sometimes substantially so in comparison to apparel that is new. There are also jobs that are created both in an industrialized nation, such as the United States and abroad in countries like Haiti or Pakistan.

As an example, my shoe drive fundraising, logistics, and recycling companies alone account for 30 people who have jobs in the United States or support our efforts around the world, including in Europe. And, as I've mentioned, these companies and brands provide business opportunities by our estimates to more than 4,000 people who are creating or maintaining their micro-businesses selling clothing and shoes.

In our country, the textile recycling industry[24] removes 2.5 billion pounds of consumer textiles from waste, which creates more than 17,000 jobs. Across the U.S. there are more than 500 recycling companies for

24   "Textile Recycling Facts and Figures," The Balance, Small Business, Rick Leblanc, September 24, 2018, https://www.thebalancesmb.com/textile-recycling-facts-and-figures-2878122

clothing, most of which are owned and operated by small business owners. In other words, recycling and repurposing make economic sense for our country and others.

Why Don't We Repurpose and Recycle More?

Most developed nations are good at recycling and repurposing—some items. For instance, we do a reasonable job of recycling glass bottles, plastics, and paper. I think it's fair to say that most communities in our country have educated the public well for the need to separate their bottles and paper from the other trash. However, while this is a start, it's not enough, and there is still so much we can be doing. The issue is that most people don't know enough, and communities have to invest much more time and resources into informing the public if we have any chance of helping the environment and all living things.

The average American throws away 80 pounds of clothing[25] annually, in the garbage. That's a tragedy not only for the environment but also for the micro-entrepreneurs around the world who could be using those clothes to sell or for the making of other products. If you do a simple search on the internet, one of the primary reasons[26] people seem to think that throwing out clothing and shoes is easier rather than giving them to a recycling or repurposing effort is because they don't know where to go. Also, in one survey, 54 percent of the public had no idea who would take their stuff, or even want it, which is an economic loss of $88 billion. You now know that that assumption is inaccurate.

Candidly, even though we live in a great nation like the United States, we can and should do more. Although our recycling rates have more than tripled in the previous 30 years, we have to do the same with clothing and shoes that we did with glass, paper, and plastics. As was noted in a recent headline by *The Saturday Evening Post*, "Ready-to-Waste: America's Clothing Crisis."

We have to create ways for every person from a big city to a rural town to understand that there is indeed use for the clothing and shoes they no longer want or need. By choosing to partner with a social enterprise in a shoe drive fundraiser or with a recycler, such as Head2Toe Recycling, we can make a significant social impact.

As I've mentioned in Chapter 2, four benefits come with being

25 "Textile Recycling Facts and Figures," The Balance, Small Business, Rick Leblanc, September 24, 2018, https://www.thebalancesmb.com/textile-recycling-facts-and-figures-2878122
26 "You're Probably Going To Throw Away 81 Pounds Of Clothing This Year," Huffington Post, Eleanor Goldberg, June 8, 2016, https://www.huffingtonpost.com/entry/youre-likely-going-to-throw-away-81-pounds-of-clothing-this-year_us_57572bc8e4b08f74f6c069d3?guccounter=1

more thoughtful with the textiles we don't need.

We can raise money for favorite charitable causes.

We can provide materials, inventory and business opportunities for small business owners in developing nations.

We help save our planet and leave our legacy in doing the right thing for our children, grand-children and future generations.

We provide work opportunities, which include American jobs, for people to provide for themselves and their families.

The next chapters will help you understand and learn how you can create something that can help you make a difference in the world. You know, I have always felt that there is no reason we have to have so much of the suffering we do. There is an opportunity in many places and ways to change not just one, but many lives. All it takes is a remembrance that we're tied together, and we share more in common than what makes us different. It takes a little creativity and a desire to do something positive.

For instance, let's take recycling. By partnering with a city, town or local government and helping people understand how they can recycle, people—perhaps someone like you—can do several things. You can become part of a movement. You can help the environment. You can earn money for a good cause, such as your favorite charity. You can do your part in creating a pipeline of clothing and shoes that are used by people in developing countries for business and commerce opportunities. You can make a significant social impact. Isn't that what it's all about? Isn't that why we're here; to do good for ourselves, but more importantly, others?

CHAPTER 7
How to Successfully Create Your Social Enterprise

"The secret to success is to know something nobody else knows."
— Aristotle Onassis

I began this book by speaking about my experience as the founder and CEO of Soles4Souls, which was followed by my journey having the shoe drive fundraising brands with Funds2Orgs Group. As I mentioned in the previous chapter, my team and I have launched Head2Toe Recycling. What I'd like to do for the final part of this section in the book is to tell you about a few of the critical decisions we've had to make in the creation of our social enterprises, including Funds2Orgs Group, as well as Head2Toe Recycling.

As you will recall, when I founded Soles4Souls, my team and I had worked on securing a $20 million start-up grant. It was a requirement that the organization had to set up as a nonprofit. However, since that time, the Funds2Orgs Group brands and now Head2Toe Recycling are all for-profit social enterprises. Social enterprises can be not-for-profit or for-profit, which are more often the case, but one thing they all share in common is that they're created to achieve a social impact.

Despite people like Dan Pallotta and others, including me, who speak publicly about paying people in the nonprofit sector competitive wages as is the norm in the for-profit world, there is also an insistence that salaries for nonprofit executives should be low because paying competitive wages somehow "wastes" money. As I have explained, it's a pathological idea within the philanthropic sector that keeps many talented people earning less than what they would be paid for similar jobs in the for-profit world.

In my experience, there's much more flexibility and acceptance for research and development in the for-profit universe, and all that involves, including failure. For-profits are expected to test and pilot ideas where in the nonprofit industry there seems to be resistance by leaders and also funders concerning innovative ideas testing and piloting because of the concern not to "waste" money." Of course, this is a mistake, but this kind of thinking is notoriously persistent in the nonprofit world.

For me, the decision is easy. If you are interested in making a difference and want the flexibility to be innovative with fewer restraints, create a for-profit social enterprise. If you're seeking to make an impact, but also want to make a profit and become a dominant player in your particular niche, establish a for-profit social enterprise. That would be my recommendation for you.

Business Planning Matters

After you've settled on an idea for a social enterprise if you want to help others and also challenge yourself in creating a business, you have to do a few things exceptionally well: 1) execute the concept; 2) develop the people in your team; and, 3) protect your brand.

When I started to think that there was another opportunity for my suite of businesses by creating a recycling brand, which ultimately became Head2Toe Recycling, and after I completed intensive research and market analysis, I moved toward creating the business plan. Unfortunately, I've seen entrepreneurs who have skipped this part because they want to build the business, and they've missed the foundational step. A business plan matters because you can't possibly execute exceptionally well, which you have to do to become the best in the industry, without having the roadmap.

From a regulatory perspective, a business plan also helps you demonstrate to the authorities that you have a real business and not a side-hobby. If your organization should ever get audited, a business plan is a benefit toward demonstrating that you have a well-thought-out concept with a roadmap and a strategy.

Secondly, when you're seeking to raise capital, if you look to do it outside of your own pocket, or that of your friends or family, you're going to have a business plan. Even if you ask for a loan from a business-minded friend, a business plan is vital in demonstrating that you're serious about what you want to do.

Your business plan will force you to think through every aspect of your business, including how to make money, and that's going to help you build your financial projections because as we all know, cash flow is always an essential aspect for any company. Your business plan should include the following elements: an executive summary, your business description, an overview of your management team, a competitive analysis, details about your product or service, your marketing plan and your financial information (e.g., financial projections, cash flow, income statements, etc.).

Legal and Tax Structures

How your for-profit business is structured can have an impact on what you're trying to achieve both in making a profit and also having a social impact. Always speak to tax and legal experts to make sure that you set up the structure well and in a compliant manner.

Although I cannot provide tax and legal counsel since I'm neither an accountant nor a lawyer, I've found that Morrison Foerster and TrustLaw Connect have created an excellent guide[27] for establishing a social enterprise. I have never worked with this company, nor do I have any relationship with them, but what they published, I thought was very easy to understand. They explained, "Legal structure can have a material impact on an entity's pursuit of this dual mission of profit and social value. The legal structure that an organization adopts sets the framework and governing rules under which it operates. Each organizational form has certain advantages and disadvantages in this respect, the materiality, and applicability of which vary depending on the characteristics of an organization."

When I create a new business, I make it a point to confer with my legal and tax advisors. Not doing so is penny-wise and pound foolish. You might think, especially when you're starting, and funds are limited, that you should just set yourself up as a sole proprietor, which I wouldn't recommend because of the personal risk in this type of structure, but there are pluses and benefits to various structures. If you're serious about your business, which you should be, one of the first most essential things you need to do is to determine the legal and tax structures of your social enterprise.

Legally, your business can be a sole proprietorship, limited

---

27 "Which Legal Structure is Right for My Social Enterprise? A Guide to Establishing a Social Enterprise in the United States," Morrison Foerster and TrustLaw Connect, http://media.mofo.com/files/uploads/Images/Guide-to-Establishing-a-Social-Enterprise.pdf

liability company (LLC), partnership (general or limited liability partnership), corporation or something else, such as a cooperative or trust.

From a tax perspective, you have the options of being a sole proprietorship, general or limited liability partnership, corporation (C corporation, S corporation, personal service corporation), or a cooperative or trust.

As you're looking to set up your social enterprise, we've done, take the time to determine both the best legal and tax structures. Also, remember, that each state has different tax structures, so you're not only going to be making this determination for IRS purposes but also your state government. As you speak to your tax and law advisors, there are four elements that you want to be sure are to your satisfaction when choosing legal and tax structures.

1. You want to limit personal liability.
2. You want to ensure you understand your tax liabilities at the federal and state/city levels.
3. You want to understand the transferability of your business in the case of incapacity, death or sale.
4. If you're looking to have partners or investors at some point, you must know how the tax and legal structures of your social enterprise affect these two objectives.

Talent, Talent, Talent
Concerning the people on your team who work for you, let's look at this in two ways. One from a leadership perspective and then from the more technical management view, which is essential for consideration as you build your company.

Do not hire for talent, knowledge or skill
We're well into the 21st Century, and so the best companies are the ones who recruit talent that is agile. Your instinct might be to review resumes and past performance of the people whom you're thinking about bringing onto your team. The first thing I'm going to tell you is that with concern to Head2Toe Recycling, and also Funds2Orgs Group, while we take a look at resumes, that's not the primary driver for us. Our management team doesn't make decisions based on a resume for talent.

Here's one of the most important "secrets" to our success. The reason we choose anyone to be on our team is that they demonstrate motivation, energy, and curiosity. While technical expertise, talent and experience help round out a professional, we've hired people who have had resumes that are not anywhere related to the job to which we've hired them. It's been the fire in their belly that has motivated us to hire them, and we've never been wrong—not a single time.

Top talent does not have the paycheck mentality

As an entrepreneur, I notice who on my team makes the extra effort and who is looking to punch the time clock. Let me tell you something; the world is very competitive. I will admit to you that people who are part of our global team of full-time, part-time, consultants and freelancers and merely seeking to earn the paycheck at the end of the week, they don't

last very long as a member of our team. We're not looking for people with paycheck mentalities.

The people who are the most successful for our social enterprises are those who are intellectually curious, driven, and motivated. They have energy that explodes out of the box. As we've moved toward the hard launch of Head2Toe Recycling, as I've written this book with Melissa, our team has been working hard, not only making sure that the business objectives of the other businesses and brands are met. Now that we also have Head2Toe Recycling on our plates, we've also had an eye on that ball. We're all stretching and doing more, but the energy is incredible.

We feel the excitement of what we're doing. We're working overtime to make sure Head2Toe Recycling gets out of the gates like the dominate runner from the moment of its launch. You see, there's not a single person on the team who does not believe that Head2Toe Recycling is not already a great success. The team has a mindset of success. Each one of us has the curiosity to learn new things. Every one of us is motivated, and we're all excited and energized about greater success, which we know will help many others around the world. I think it's fair to say that we all understand that we're tied together.

Between all of our team members located in different places around the world, including Orlando, Florida, Tennessee, Europe, the Caribbean, and Asia, someone on our international team is doing something work-related—literally—24 hours a day, 7 days a week, 365 days a year. So, to work with a dedicated group of people like that, you have to have a fair amount of rock stars who are always seeking to do more, for the company, the team, themselves and for the work we do around the world. How does that happen? How do we get such vibrant energy? We hire for the potential, not for the past performance.

Potential is the essential quality for talent in the 21ˢᵗ Century
Argentinian author and global talent and leadership expert for more than thirty years, Claudio Fernández-Aráoz, who is also ranked as one of the top executive search consultants in the world, has written about potential. One day at the end of last year, I posted on social media how potential, motivation and energy were the essential qualities for new talent. As I was writing this book, and because I'm a student of leadership, I researched the topic and fell upon Claudio Fernández-Aráoz, who provided my instincts with the academic thought.

He has outlined in the *Harvard Business Review*[28] his thinking of modern hiring practices for talent, which is a fascinating explanation of recruiting. Fernández-Aráoz has explained the selection process for talent as being encapsulated into four eras, which are as follows:

1. **Physical attributes drive recruitment.** Fernández-Aráoz explains that since the beginning of time with humans on this planet, the primary way that selection had been done for a job has been with physical attributes. For millennia, it's been necessary to hire people based on their physical characteristics to cultivate crops, fight wars, or to build bridges, homes, and buildings.

28   "21st-Century Talent Spotting," Harvard Business Review, Claudio Fernández-Aráoz, https://hbr.org/2014/06/21st-century-talent-spotting

2. **Experience, intelligence and past performance for talent selection.** Finally, along came the 20th Century and for most of that time, the selection process for new team members was based on past performance, education, and testing. It was during modern times that work was professionalized and the people who were selected for the top positions were intelligent individuals who had demonstrated proficiency in the past based on what they had done.

3. **Competency for recruitment.** As the 20th Century began to draw to a close in the 1980s and as leaders began to look at the dawn of a new century and millennia, competency became the driving factor of the selection process because the world was becoming more complex. Businesses needed to have talent that had the right mix of skills and characteristics that were the competencies necessary for doing the work that needed to get done.

4. **Volatile, uncertain, complex and ambiguous environment (VUCA).** As Fernández-Aráoz noted, VUCA is a military term, which has been adopted by corporations. Because the world is now extraordinarily complex, rapidly evolving, uncertain, and volatile, competencies are no longer the necessary approach for leaders seeking talent. What is now essential is the potential for talent. As Fernández-Aráoz noted in his article, "What makes someone successful in a particular role today might not tomorrow if the competitive environment shifts, the company's strategy changes, or he or she must collaborate with or manage a different group of colleagues. So the question is not whether your company's employees and leaders have the right skills; it's whether they have the potential to learn new ones."[29]

In his follow-up article, *"Turning Potential into Success: The Missing Link in Leadership Development,"*[30] for *Harvard Business Review*, Fernández-Aráoz addresses how to ensure you're focused on the development of the people on your team who demonstrate potential, motivation, energy and intellectual curiosity. Based on the article, the following are the elements for developing leaders. Although they are driven toward large corporations, successful entrepreneurs understand that these elements can also be adapted, especially for talent, for small businesses and social enterprises.

29 "21st-Century Talent Spotting," Harvard Business Review, Claudio Fernández-Aráoz, https://hbr.org/2014/06/21st-century-talent-spotting

30 "Turning Potential into Success: The Missing Link in Leadership Development," Harvard Business Review, Claudio Fernández-Aráoz, Andrew Roscoe, Kentaro Aramaki, https://hbr.org/2017/11/turning-potential-into-success-the-missing-link-in-leadership-development

1. The seven qualities for leadership success of talent are, "results orientation, strategic orientation, collaboration and influence, team leadership, developing organizational capabilities, change leadership, *and* market understanding." Fernández-Aráoz also adds inclusiveness to the mix.
2. Rating performance for aspiring managers should be done based on the following criteria, "curiosity, insight, engagement and determination."[31]
3. Leaders want to create a growth map which demonstrates how someone's strengths in curiosity, insight, engagement, and determination, which are called "hallmarks" align with the competencies of the job.
4. The people who demonstrate high potential should have their jobs rotated and should experience promotions to which they might not seem qualified, but because of their growth map, they can be coached and developed into the new roles.

Creating an environment of high-expectations and performance is essential for a social enterprise or business. We're not going back to a time when everything was regular and certain. Because we live in a dynamic world and do business with so many factors having to change based on information that is continually evolving, having the right people on board—those who demonstrate potential, curiosity, intellect, and motivation—is essential.

Your Name is Your Brand, Take the Time to Think Carefully
One of the most famous stories in naming a company is that of Google, which we know is one of the top five global companies as the largest search engine in the world. Initially, when Larry Page began the company with Sergey Bring, the company that we know today as Google was called Back-Rub. After one year in business, the team decided to change the name from a noun to a verb and rebranded the company to be called Google, which better suited what they envisioned for the company. If Page and Bring had not changed the name, we would be talking about "Backrubbing" a search instead of "Googling" it.

The point of this story is that brand matters, and you want to make everything related to it right, including the name. For many years, I've known that people remember numbers, so you'll see the companies and brands generally follow the pattern, Funds2Orgs, Sneakers4Funds and

---

31 21st-Century Talent Spotting," Harvard Business Review, Claudio Fernández-Aráoz, https://hbr.org/2014/06/21st-century-talent-spotting

now Head2Toe Recycling. If you look at each of the names, the entire message of what we do is captured.

Funds2Orgs: This time we wanted to align the idea of fundraising for organizations such as nonprofits, churches, schools, and civic groups.

Sneakers4Funds: When we created this brand, we wanted the focus to be on athletic shoes, and we sought to connect sneakers to money, or funds.

Head2Toe Recycling: The wordplay here was the fact that if someone could imagine the clothes and the footwear being worn and recycled.

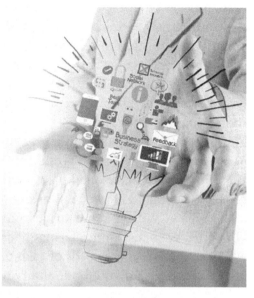

Each time we were developing a new brand, my team and I thought long and hard about the name, which meant that we had to have clarity around the entirety of the business. Once we felt comfortable with the products and services the company would provide, as well as the benefits to our customers and partners, we spent weeks, if not months, working through names that evoked what the company did.

When you're in the process of thinking about the development of your social enterprise, you've got to do the same thing, especially when you're a small business. Everything about your brand identity has to be *memorable*.

Protect Your Brand Image and Name

My marketing team and I, as well as everyone else associated with representing the businesses and brands, are relentless about protecting the brands. Once we determine the positioning of each of the brands, we do not deviate unless we're doing so strategically or for a specific reason, such as a rebrand, which we did with the Cash4Shooz brand earlier this year.

Unfortunately, especially in the age of social media, you might find yourself experiencing what we've faced, which has been individuals and companies trying to steal the identities of our brands. I've mentioned that we're relentless in protecting our brands, and that means that we monitor it diligently every day, 365 days of the year. We continually check that our websites are functioning correctly, and we watch for the creation of any fake social media accounts or pages that might be developed using our brand images.

Internally, we have brand guidelines, which include every detail about brand positioning. It covers everything from the exact PMS colors to the precise language we use for SEO. Nothing is left to chance, and when it happens, as it will from time to time on any team, that we see or hear our team members misrepresenting one of our brands or mentioning something that does not agree with our positioning, we nip it in the bud. Your brand is your identity and just like your name or digital presence, you don't want it stolen or misrepresented.

I want to make one final note that I think is important for you to consider, especially if you're someone who sees the development of different niches. With the shoe drive fundraising brands under Funds2Orgs Group, we've focused on offering diverse niches, different product lines, which are based on the needs of each particular segment. We've done this because it's only enhanced our ability to gain market share, and candidly, either buy or be far superior to what our competitors offer.

Every one of the brands under Funds2Orgs Group does shoe drive fundraising, but we've differentiated each brand, and it's allowed us to

dominate the industry by absorbing up market share.

Funds2Orgs is the original company and primarily partners with nonprofits, churches, civic groups and companies.

Sneakers4Funds differentiates itself with athletic shoe drive fundraisers primarily partnering with running and sports clubs, mud runs, road races, retail stores, and individuals.

Shoes With Heart is all about the love, and we partner in this brand with families in need of funds of money for adoptions, service animals, or medical needs. We also work with veterans and small community grassroots organizations, such as homeless or domestic shelters.

Cash4Shooz is about fundraising for schools and education.

Internally, we have documents and brand guidelines that explain each in detail, so there is no confusion and especially when we have new members who join our team. I can't stress this enough. Your brand identity is a commodity, and you have to protect it. It is precious and if you see bad actors, especially as you become successful, look to steal it, you have to act decisively. When you have team members divert from the brand positioning, make it a point to re-inform and re-educate. It's vital always to keep everyone on point concerning your social enterprise.

One final thing you will likely want to consider with your brand name and image is trademarking with the U.S. Patent and Trademark Office. By trademarking your name and essential aspects of your work, perhaps the way you produce one of your products or something that is a trade secret, you protect your company in the entire United States. If you ever end up in court with someone who was looking to steal your brand, especially if it is successful, your trademark will provide you with immeasurable protection.

Now that we've discussed the elements necessary for a social enterprise business, the next chapter is going to address two things that are crucial for success: money and mindset. Your perspective and relationship with money will be what stands between you and success in helping yourself, your family and also others through social enterprise creation and development.

CHAPTER 8
Mind and Money Matter

"People say that money is not the key to happiness, but I always figured if you have enough money, you can have a key made."
— **Joan Rivers, Comedian**

In the previous chapter, we discussed some of the most crucial elements of creating a successful social enterprise. When I created every single one of my businesses and brands, including the most recent company, Head2Toe Recycling, I've addressed all of these topics and more.

If you're new to being a social entrepreneur, many excellent resources can help guide you in the establishment of a business. The following are just a few of them.

- Small Business Administration
- Business News Daily
- Start Your Own Business – USAGov

I mentioned that to have success in business, you need execution and talent that is consistent and motivated. However, before you even begin to think about establishing a social enterprise, you need two other things as an entrepreneur. I talk about these two things all of the time because they're fundamental to being able to get off the couch as the owner of a company or for-profit social enterprise.

1. You need an entrepreneur mindset.
2. You need to have an exceptional relationship with money.

When you decide that you're going to jump into creating a social enterprise business, you'll find yourself facing yourself. Inevitably, unless you have a personal trust fund or have a lot of money stashed away, your mind is necessarily going to think about money. Your mindset and relationship with money will be essential to pushing through any worry or doubt.

Funding Your Social Enterprise Business

As I've mentioned, when I got started with Soles4Souls, we were fortunate to have secured fairly quickly a grant. Candidly, it was a game-changer because we knew from the start that we would be able to make a substantial investment in everything we needed to get the nonprofit organization off the ground with an incredible and thundering bang. Often, when you start a new business, you have to make compromises and prioritize how you're going to spend the money to get it successfully off the ground.

However, when I started str@tegic and then Funds2Orgs, I decided to bootstrap it. I didn't pay myself a salary for years because I didn't want to take a loan. Every brand I've created with my team since has been done

with my own money, and any credit lines I've received for any particular business have been repaid promptly. I shy away from debt, and I'm going to tell you why you should as well.

Perhaps you've dreamed about starting your own business or for-profit social enterprise, and as you've read the pages of this book, you've thought to yourself that you can do what my team and I have done. You want to meet people and change their lives. If that's your dream, then do it. Get serious, develop the plan and then consistently execute. Be like the horse with the blinders on with relentless focus seeking to dominate the field down the straightaway before passing through the finish line as the winner.

I love the challenge of making money and you should as well. You have to have a good relationship with it. If you have it as your enemy or something that is a limited resource in your life, then it's hard to be positive about it, which is essential for success. I wrote about that idea extensively in my book, *Get Off the Couch: Grip & Rip and Break the Barriers Holding You Back in Life*.[32]

I've also mentioned the importance of curiosity. Even though I've achieved a lot in my life, there's always more to do, and there's certainly more to learn. Being restless helps, especially when you want to change the world.

Not too long ago, I read an article[33] written by Michael Kay about money that I enjoyed so much that I posted it on social media because it was very much aligned with how I thought about money. Kay wrote about several strategies for having a stronger relationship with money.

1. Become intentional.
2. Set realistic goals.
3. Track your progress.
4. Learn how to talk about money without starting a war.

Money is an essential fact in our lives, and I'm going to tell you that if you don't get comfortable with money and not having a fear of having it, losing it, or having a passive-aggressive relationship with it, you're not going to succeed. If you're an entrepreneur, you have to enjoy the opportunity to make money, as much as you enjoy the thought of making a social impact as a social entrepreneur. If you want to be a social entrepreneur, you have to not only enjoy the challenge of making money, but you also have to like the idea of figuring out innovative ways to improve the world for others. Those two ideas have to occupy the space in your mind, at the same time.

Paycheck Versus Winner's Mentality
You know the paycheck mentality. People like that only care about the money in the bank on Friday, which is typically spent by Monday. Successful people do not have the paycheck mentality even if they work for someone else; they have a mindset that is all about winning, being the best and dominating in business, including with money.

32   "Get Off the Couch: Grip & Rip and Break the Barriers Holding You Back in Life," Wayne Elsey, 2015, https://www.amazon.com/Get-Off-Couch-Barriers-Holding/dp/057816910X/ref=sr_1_1?ie=UT-F8&qid=1542393262&sr=8-1&keywords=wayne+elsey+get+off+the+couch
33   "Strengthening Your Relationship with Money Can Lead to Living Your Most Valued Life," Inc., Michael Kay, October 18, 2018, https://www.inc.com/michael-kay/why-your-personal-relationship-with-money-can-help-you-live-the-good-life.html?fbclid=IwAR3_rlaShUSmzCBxgKu0RPqHSziOyrSRT52x4RUq_eqGi-1djkOakeskaf-M

One of the questions I'm often asked is how I developed multiple companies and brands after I left Soles4Souls without a paycheck and with my own money. With the fact that more than 50 percent of businesses fail before the fifth year in business, I knew that I faced significant odds. However, I looked at the odds not from the point of failure but the view of success. I don't see failure as a bad thing; it's only an experience for learning and people from Albert Einstein to the world's leading CEOs of today have spoken about failing thousands of time, often, and failing fast. There's always learning to be done in failure, which will eventually bring you success, but only if you're consistent and keep chipping away and making the necessary adjustments.

Since most people work, I think the toughest moment will arise when you're faced with the decision of leaving the paycheck to invest 100 percent of your time into the social enterprise. I've been faced with that moment, and countless other entrepreneurs have as well. When I left Soles4Souls, I had a stark choice. I could return to the corporate world where I'd had enormous success, or I could dive right into starting a new venture. I thought about it for a little bit, but for me, my destiny had already been set because I've always had an entrepreneurial spirit.

When I decided to establish str@tegic, I just knew it in my bones that I was going to be successful. Although it was uncomfortable not to pay myself a salary for years, I had a home, and I knew that with the team I had by my side, I was going to be very successful. It wasn't so much a matter of if, but when. It happened within five years, which seems to be the magic number for me, and again, I find myself as the CEO of a portfolio of multi-million dollar social enterprise businesses and brands. All of this started with an idea and a team that met and worked off a kitchen table to now become a sizable company.

I do understand the security found in a paycheck, but when the moment arrives that realize that you can't do your social enterprise business as a side hustle, you'll want to be as confident as I was that you will succeed. The only way to be that certain, especially if you've never started your own successful business before is to have done all of the preparation in advance by getting your business plan in order. You also need to have made sure you've got about nine months to a year of financial reserves in the instance that you do not earn money, so you're not running back for a job.

Ultimately, I think you will have to make the jump to become an entrepreneur full-time for two reasons. 1) You can't succeed with only part of your body in the water—you have to get into the pool fully; and, 2) If your mind is elsewhere, instead of your job, you're not going to be productive at the work you're doing for someone else. As a businessman, if you've got a side hustle that's taking up your time to the extent that another business does, you're not going to be working to the top of your talent and potential for me. I don't mind if people on my team have other pursuits; for instance, I have someone who works for me who does theater. I do care if someone has a business they're trying to get off the ground, and they're doing it on my dime. A person who does that has a paycheck mentality, and they'll never be a successful entrepreneur because they're afraid to take the risk by taking the plunge fully with careful planning.

Ways to Fund Your Business
As I've mentioned, I don't like debt, and many of the small business owners who own very successful multi-million dollar companies have funded their companies. If they've borrowed, they've obtained loans for small amounts and sought to pay it back as quickly as possible. While debt can be strategically used, it can be easy to get into problems. Treat debt with all of the deference it deserves. Remember, it's not your money; it's someone else's money. So, when you use someone else's money, only borrow a little and pay it back *before* it is due.

There are two primary types of financing for considering when the moment comes for you to establish your company.

1. **Debt financing** is where you borrow money to get your company off the ground. Again, although many businesses get started with debt financing, it's not your money, and whether or not you succeed, you're going to have to pay it back, usually with interest.
2. **Equity financing** is when you give someone else a share or partial ownership of your business in return for money. Often, friends, family or investors help finance companies with an equity stake.

The way I believe is the best way to fund your business is by bootstrapping it. Personally, I thrive on the challenges of growing a business, and I don't like partners or investors in my companies, as much as I enjoy and like people. I prefer to keep things as uncomplicated as possible, and my preference is to minimize or not take on any debt.

There's No Money Out There for You

If you take a look at news articles about starting your own business, there are countless headlines and pieces written about getting funding. By the sound of it, people make it sound as if it's raining money for investments when the reality is quite the opposite. If you're reading this book and thinking that you have a brilliant idea, which I'm sure it is, and you're going to get someone to invest in it, the chances are high, that's not going to happen. The vast majority of start-ups, including social enterprises, receive zero start-up funds.

Why does it appear as if everyone getting investment money?

Because news media has to get you to click and read their articles. It's fake news.

The chances of your getting a loan or investment capital, especially with no track record of success, which was why I got the $20 million grant with my team, is close to zero. Also, if you choose to try to apply for a loan, your personal credit score is going to matter, so if you go down that road, you'll want to be sure that you have a score higher than 700 if and when you want to see if you can get a small loan.

The reality is that you'll discover, if you haven't already, that the only time lenders or investors want to give you money or extend you a line of credit is when you have a lot of money. Why? You're a much safer bet when you have money. When you don't have money, the only lenders you'll probably find are predatory lenders with usury rates. It's only another reason why you should get yourself into the mindset of bootstrapping. In the end, although it seems like a high mountain to climb, the people who aren't extending you any credit or a loan are doing you a favor. You don't want to find yourself in a hole.

However, if you want to learn about funds that are out there for some point down the line, perhaps in your second year when you want to do a little expansion, I'll provide you with several ideas and resources to look into in your research.

1. **Personal assets:** If you're serious about creating a business or for-profit social enterprise that is going to succeed, as I've mentioned, bootstrapping it is the best way to go. You might have more financial assets than you realize beyond simply your savings account. Assess everything, from the equity in your home to your retirement savings. Take the time to sit with financial and tax advisors who are experts in helping you deal with any taxation or penalty issues (especially if you're dealing with retirement accounts).

2. **Family loans:** I don't think asking your friends and family, especially mom or dad, for money is a good idea because it can be a contentious issue, especially if there are differing expectations. Still, some people ask their family or good friends to help them get a business off the ground. If you're going to make this approach, I would suggest giving them a small equity stake in the company. Also, when you present to them and ask them for the loan (as little as possible), present your business plan and treat it like a business arrangement, which it is, between you and them. Finally, formalize it with a written agreement or contract that will delineate terms and a repayment plan.

3. **Small Business Administration:** You would think that the SBA is in the business of making loans, but it isn't. It's in the business of facilitating loans, through third parties, that have the highest possibility of getting repaid. They also help with grants for research and development. To see about obtaining an SBA loan, take a look at their website or go to your local bank to see if you could get an SBA loan through them as a third-party lender.

4. **Peer-to-Peer Lenders:** For loans that can be as little as only a couple of thousand dollars to as much as $40,000, peer-to-peer lenders may be a good option. Two of the more renowned peer-to-peer lenders where borrowers and lenders are connected, and loans are paid in between three to five years, are Lending Club and Prosper.

Even if you create a social enterprise where you're excited about working toward making the world a better place, you're still running a business, and the success of what you're doing relies on the profit you and your team make. If you can't get your social enterprise off the ground financially, it doesn't matter what you want to do for others; you won't be able to get it done because you don't have the money and resources.

Again, although I wrote about where you can find investment or start-up funds, my approach has always been to borrow little, if anything, and do it with your own resources. That said, the more important takeaway from this section is that you have to have a healthy relationship with money. That means you have to be able to speak about it, be real about it, not be afraid of money and get very familiar with it.

Creating a business or social enterprise takes a lot of work, dedication, and drive, but it's not impossible to do. There are times when I'm pensive and reflective and am humbled and awed at what people who have believed as I do, that we're all tied together, have been able to create and develop starting with Soles4Souls to Funds2Orgs Group and now, our latest venture, Head2Toe Recycling. It's been years of hard work, but I sleep well each night knowing that we're working as a collective group for goals that extend beyond profit and seek to improve the lives and circumstances of people in this world. The road hasn't been created magically. As I've said, it's been work, but it's also been a collective passion for bigger things in the hope of developing sustainable social enterprise brands and providing opportunities for people in our country and around the world.

Tied Together in Hope Means Doing More, Rewards Will Follow
At this stage, my thoughts about business are drawing to a close for this book, and we're going to shift gears with Melissa's section, which begins in the next chapter. As I mentioned, when I set out to write this book, I

had not yet experienced the incredible and humbling response of so many who sent words of kindness, generosity, and support for the efforts that my team and I have done to make the world a better place.

Reading the stories, reflections and endorsements brought memories, smiles and warmed my heart. Strangely, it was like attending my funeral without having died, thankfully, to have so many people send heartfelt thoughts about what they've experienced with me.

It's time to share their words with you, which is an honor for me. Melissa will guide you on this next part of the journey and reflect on what she read. If she knew the person personally or heard me speak about them, she'll help add a bit of context to the words they shared.

Again, we're all human.

We're all one, and we're more the same than we are different.

One of the lessons that came out of this experience is that if you put positive energy out into the world, it will return to you. That's what happened when we were flooded with hundreds of emails and support.

I'll be forever grateful for having experienced it and having taken the time to read through what many had to say. I can only wish this type of experience on you as well. It makes all of the work, and life, worthwhile.

PART II
Memories & Reflection

CHAPTER 9
YOU Matter; A Legacy

*"Carve your name on hearts, not tombstones. A legacy is etched into the
minds of others and the stories they share about you."*
— **Shannon L. Alder**

The first part of this book my dad wrote can serve as an illustration or road
map for you that reminds us that anyone can make a difference. Being
kind and making the world a better place can begin with a simple smile.
Impacting someone's life can mean lending a shoulder to lean on for a
friend or listening. Making a positive difference can be making a donation or volunteering for a cause that's dear to your heart. It can also be
creating something like my dad has done with his teams when he founded
Soles4Souls and then developed Funds2Orgs Group. The one action that
is required is that we have the intent to do it and then show-up each day
working toward making the world a better place.

As my dad mentioned at the beginning of this book, during the
holidays, he asked people he knew to share their thoughts, reflections or
stories about their experience with him, the book or the work he's done. If
you know my father, as motivated as he can be in his work, he's also someone who allows people to do what they think is best and then he incorpo-
rates their ideas into his thinking, or in this case, into a book.

When my father shared with me the endorsements, stories, memories, and reflections that people sent, I noticed he was moved. Once I
started to read some of the material myself, I too couldn't help but also feel
a bit of the emotion that he felt. I think of my dad as the guy who would
make it a point to take me to the Ritz-Carlton for Shirley Temple, while
he pretended to have something stronger. Here's a secret; my dad is not
much of a drinker. He doesn't drink much coffee, and he barely likes the
taste of alcohol. But still, those dates with my father at the Ritz were special
because of the time I spent with him and the conversations we had about
whatever was on my mind. He's the same guy who's doing it all over again

with his granddaughter, Aubree.

We all walk through this world, and we hope that we can make a positive impact on someone's life. What happened when my dad received the hundreds of emails was that, for the first time, he saw what his work and he meant to so many people. Yes, I think it's fair to say that he was able to see what others viewed as his legacy, and that's probably an experience that not a lot of people have while living.

As he mentioned, at the start of the book, while this experience was humbling, the fountain of support he received in words submitted by so many people created a challenge for how to integrate the content with what he had written. He never wanted this book to be about him.

If you know my dad, although he's someone who is very confident, he's also one of the best listeners. For instance, in meetings, which I've had the opportunity to see him lead, he's the person who will say the least and listen the most.

The discussions about what to do about the book with so much content from others who were his supporters began with the family, including Courtney, Josh and me. We spoke about what to do with the generosity of thought, words, and spirit that had been shared for my dad. As we reflected on my father's life and experience, there were a few themes that became apparent. First and foremost, we saw that family, followed by friendships and relationships with others were themes in what people sent.

My dad is all about family first. Even when members of his team have family issues, unlike perhaps other managers, he is the person who will give someone the space they need to deal with whatever happens. He understands that people have lives outside of the work environment. Closely entwined with the idea of the family are friends. My dad is the guy who will always be there to support and help someone and never expect anything in return.

Thirdly, his life is about his work. He's had the opportunity to work in the shoe business since he was 15 years old and now, in his 50s, he's still in the shoe business. He may no longer be leading global shoe manufacturing companies, but he's still in the shoe business. He's taken his passion for shoes and figured out how to create a nonprofit, Soles4Souls, that has helped people around the world for many years.

Once he moved on to create what's become Funds2Orgs Group, he was able to broaden the idea of what shoes can do. They can not only help micro-entrepreneurs around the world, provide a way for all of us to do our part for the planet, but he also developed businesses that have created jobs right here in the U.S. and has helped thousands of organizations, businesses, and families raise money. Candidly, I think that's quite a feat of business smarts, not to mention his activities in real estate, logistics and his strategic marketing company, which is another passion for him.

When I started looking at how to organize all of the kind words provided by so many people, it occurred to me that once we gathered the endorsements, many people in my dad's life had been co-workers or folks he met along the way, but whom he ultimately considers friends. Some of the people I've personally met, and others I haven't, but I'll offer my thoughts, as well as throw a few fun-loving digs at my dad because that's what we do, and it keeps him human and always approachable. No matter what we achieve in life, we're all human, and we all want love, laughter, and joy.

Voices of Family and Friends

Francis J. Venincasa, or "Fran," was my dad's best pal. When Fran was diagnosed with cancer, he was given a 10 percent chance at survival, which is devastating news for anyone. It would have been easy for Fran to focus on the 90 percent chance that he was going to die soon. Instead, Fran decided to work the percentages, and he chose to focus on the 10 percent chance he had at surviving beyond one year.

After his diagnosis, Fran lived another 10 years with cancer, and he died in 2012 at the age of 80. His wife, Katherine Hamelin, whom my dad also loves very much sent kind words to my father. Katherine is considered family.

I can't overestimate how much my father still remembers Fran. I can attest to the fact that when my dad is going through something, he often reflects on what Fran would say if he were sitting with him. Fran was a dominant force in my dad's like, and still is, which is evidence of the impact any one of us can make on someone else. We may not ever know it, but we should all never forget that others may remember us. The impression we make can be positive, or negative, and it's ours to choose how we want to be remembered.

"My late husband and I met Wayne some 14 years ago. As I look back on that meeting and think about being 'tied together' as humans, I can't help but think that there is no one better at that than Wayne. Wayne can tie together the most eclectic group of people at any gathering. Like a box of chocolates, you never know who you will find in Wayne's world.

Wayne makes an impact in lives across the board, enriching them socially and economically, from the chance encounter with the Uber driver to a planned meeting with a CEO of a large company, from his 94-year-old best lady friend to a couple starting a life together. His reach is broad and his impact, resonating.

Although my husband isn't with us anymore, Wayne, in his ever busy life, always keeps him alive in our hearts and minds. He is part of every social event, conversation, and joke. Thirty years Wayne's senior, Fran imparted his life lessons and 'Franisms' on Wayne; Fran color blind in a world he found colorful and hopeful, Wayne anxious and attentive to the lessons.

Fran's favorite, 'What a Wonderful World'...The colors of the rainbow so pretty in the sky are also on the faces of people going by. I see friends shaking hands saying how do you do. They're really saying I love you." – **Katherine Hamelin**

Another fantastic person who sent my dad words of support is Amber Thompson. She's also a cousin of mine and an awesome family member.

Again, we have an instance where someone makes a significant impact on someone's life, although the person might not realize it. Amber's dad, Jimmy, is also a fantastic human being, and he has had an enormous impact on my dad with his positive reinforcement. Candidly, I'm not sure if even Amber realizes how much my dad still loves and appreciates her father.

Jimmy supports my dad in anything and everything he has ever done. Sometimes his support was not asked, but nevertheless, Jimmy has been there giving my dad whatever he has needed. My dad has great memories of Jimmy and his daughter, Amber, has picked up a lot of his traits.

"I first remember meeting Wayne when I was a little girl. My dad, Wayne's 'favorite' uncle, took me to visit Wayne to procure a pair of shoes at the store he managed. Here stood this extraordinarily tall and good-humored man who was so full of life and laughter. Wayne had far more to offer me than a pair of shoes.

Even as a small child, I somehow knew that I mattered to Wayne, that I was individually special. Yes, he was a fantastic salesman who sold us a pair of amazing shoes, but the shoe sale mattered little to him ultimately. One of Wayne's strengths was seeing the customer as much more than a number. He saw each person as an individual. He cared more for the person wearing the shoes than the shoes themselves. Though we left that day with a new pair of shoes, I left with the reaffirmation that I was indeed a very special girl who happened to now possess a pair of fantastic shoes.

Fast forward thirty-five years and Wayne is still steadfastly growing businesses while being intentional in recognizing each individual as valued and essential. As Wayne so often states, 'YOU Matter.'" – **Amber Thompson**

When I was young, my dad was in the process of building Soles4Souls. I was aware of the trips that he was taking to developing nations, such as Haiti and I remember the tremendous sense of energy that permeated through our home.

I might have been young, but I was able to sense that magic was in the process of creating itself. As a child, I think one of the things that parents often miss is that seeing our moms and dads doing big things in life, sets an example that we can do it in our lives as well.

As Ryanne Cody writes in the next reflection, I'm also reminded that when we're kind and aware of others, recognizing their humanity, those little experiences are not forgotten. As my dad always says, "YOU Matter," and Ryanne is an example of that simple recognition.

"The first time I heard of Wayne was on the local news. He

was out with Soles4Souls putting shoes on children in the area. Most of these children came from low-income areas in Nashville. I was struck by his compassion for people in need around the world. For the first time, I saw someone on TV speak words about similar beliefs in charity work. Most people I have met argue that needs have to be taken care of at home first or I hear the opposite about how great the needs are of those far away. I have always felt like both mattered and when I heard him say the same thing, I knew this charity was special.

I don't remember how or when I met Wayne in person. It was just organic. I remember interacting with him on social media, and he always responded to my comments. I do remember going by the new Soles4Souls building for a grand opening celebration. There were a few other events in the area that I went to show my support and, of course, I wanted to drop off shoes, but I think one of the coolest times was I ran into him was randomly at Whole Foods.

He was having dinner at the little cafe in the back with a friend and colleague. Me being the quiet, shy, introvert, focus on my shopping list type of person that I am was stunned when he said hello. I often don't think people remember or see me, but he did. I think I was surprised because we had only talked a handful of times before and he meets many people. How could he remember little ole me? Well, he did. Moments like that make an impact. He doesn't dismiss anyone, and I think this is one of his many amazing qualities. I could go on, but I might also end up writing a book.

I look forward to reading Wayne's new book. I know it will teach me so many great lessons." – **Ryanne Cody**

Charlie Liberge and my dad worked together, a hundred years ago as my dad would say, at Stride Rite. I remember when I was a kid, my mom would host dinners for their clients. One of the most fun experiences, which I thoroughly enjoyed, was the opportunity as a child to model the shoes that my dad and his team were selling.

I loved the chance to put the shoes my dad would be selling on my feet and then serve as part of my dad's workgroup modeling the shoes for the management team of Stride Rite. I loved it, and I remember wanting to try every pair of shoes that my dad brought home with enthusiasm and happiness.

However, my dad only had sample sizes on-hand, and I would model the shoe, whether it was the right size or not. It didn't matter then. As a parent today, I understand the stories that my dad has conveyed to me of the many children he has met who must wear shoes that don't correctly fit because their parents can't afford to buy new ones for them. It is a tragedy and is one of the reasons that I'm so supportive of the work that my dad and his team do every day to serve as a bridge between groups in our country and people in developing countries who develop businesses selling shoes and families who buy the shoes for low prices for their children.

"I have known Wayne Elsey for over 25 years and closely followed his career and personal growth. My earliest memories of Wayne are one of a man possessed with being the best he could be while simultaneously motivating and encouraging those around him. In my opinion, Wayne's new book is a culmination of his vast experiences as well as his genuine care for others. Our world today seems to lack direction, focus, and compassion. Given the unending growth of technology, society has continued to distance itself from personal communication and at times is focused far too much on what immediately impacts themselves. In addition, far too much time is spent worrying about the impact others may have on you instead of thinking about how you could positively impact others.

Wayne's ability to touch other people's lives in a positive and thoughtful manner is lacking in today's world. I am sure this book and the teachings which may follow will continue to create an assurance that all is not lost and the generations of today, if presented with the opportunity and the know-how can leave behind a legacy of faith, promise, and hope for all who follow." – **Charles Liberge, PDC Fashion Group, Principal**

My dad was never someone who felt helpless in almost any situation. However, I understood that he struggled with what he could do. As the scope of the events became clear, I saw first-hand how his mind started to process how he could help in any way he could.

When the 2004 Indian Ocean tsunami hit the Pacific countries, I was a teen. I was with my dad watching the news on the television, like so many millions of others and I remember how he was moved. I saw within him, or perhaps it's better stated to say that I sensed, a shift. That event was monumental for the people affected, and I saw how my dad empathized with what was happening.

Although I've never met Joseph Dulaney personally, I've realized that my dad's story of the single shoe washing ashore in the Pacific after the tsunami made an impression on him. Joseph's words express the reality that we all want to be connected and help others when possible. We're all tied together, and I can relate to Joseph's thoughts about sharing the journey.

"I began to see Wayne's vision and social entrepreneurship first hand in December of 2004 on the Sunday following the tragedy in Sri Lanka. At our church in Nashville TN, Wayne and I began to chat at a cafe table about an 'idea' he had. He shared his story of a single shoe and with more passion than I had seen with anyone, began to lay out his idea. It was very soon after Soles4Souls was born. At that moment, I saw his vision and passion and have been lucky to be able to share in the journey along the way. Little did I know at that time, however, was that I was witnessing the launch of an amazing path, multiple organizations, and life change in many corners of the world." – **Joseph Dulaney, Educational Technology Sales Executive**

I have also never met Dan Duffy but have heard how he and my dad are close on social media and in life. I know that from time to time Dan, my dad and Courtney get together to share laughs and a good time over drinks or dinner.

124

Sometimes events or life experiences can move people, such as my dad or Dan, to create something for others. And sometimes, it's only a voice that is in someone's heart, which reverberates louder and louder until it's brought to reality.

Dan accompanied my dad to Haiti to document it. After arriving back in the U.S. and experiencing all of the devastation, Dan did a shoe drive fundraiser, starting with his son's school. He too felt compelled to make a difference. And, once he was diagnosed with cancer, I know from my dad that Dan overcame it and decided to share what he learned by creating an incredible supporting organization called The Half Fund.

I realize that people who have a disease, such as cancer, should never be defined by it because that is only an element of an entire human life. However, I also know how my dad has been impressed by Dan's courage and big vision.

Dan had stage 3 testicular cancer, and after beating it, he wrote *The Half Book: He's Taking His Ball and Going Home*, which is a testament to his courage in finding hope after a diagnosis that nearly destroyed him and the relationships in his life.

> "As a video producer, I've been so fortunate to see and film some amazing things, but nothing will ever compare with the ninety-six hours I spent in Haiti with Wayne Elsey and Todd Newton, delivering shoes to so many children in need via Soles4Souls. The stories that we captured are still so vivid in my mind.
>
> Nothing prepares you for Haiti. It's everything and nothing you think it is. For starters, the people could not be friendlier, and in many instances, happier, which very much surprised me. The city of Port-au-Prince is crowded, many of the roads aren't actually made of asphalt, and some of the poverty you see is shocking, both figuratively and literally. As we left the airport and headed to our hotel, I was messing with my camera trying to get a shot in the rapidly fading January sun. While I was trying to find the low-light sensor, Wayne tapped my leg and pointed out the window of our truck. In the haze of the dusk, I saw my first tent city and a jolt of electricity coursed through my body. I had seen poverty before while filming in some of the most urban and deeply rural places in America, but those conditions were a paradise compared to what I saw at that moment.

People were living in those tents; men, women, children, and it was dark—so dark. There were no lights. There was no sanitation. Yet, here they were, carrying on with their lives because this was the hand they were dealt. And while the people knew many of the conditions were abysmal, they kept going. They didn't use their lot in life as a crutch, and they didn't complain. Seeing this taught me a lot about who I was, and who I wanted to become.

On the Friday when we were there, a group of maybe twenty of us, left the hustle and bustle of Port-Au-Prince and traveled into the mountains outside of the city. I was

awestruck by the beauty of my current locale; the mountains were steep and lush, and the air was sweet. Had I been dropped here as my first experience in Haiti, I would wonder why it was not one of the most sought-after tourist destinations on the planet. But knowing where we'd just been not twenty minutes prior, it was always in the back of my mind that while stunningly beautiful, this country was still ravaged two years after the earthquake decimated everything in sight.

We pulled into what seemed to be a residential neighborhood. We got out of our truck and walked down the hill, where the Soles4Souls volunteers were already at our destination: an orphanage for children whose parents had died in the earthquake. Some of these kids were biological siblings, but most were connected through the same tragic loss of their moms and dads. The place was basically three large sturdily-built tents. One housed girls, one was for the boys, and one was used as both their makeshift kitchen and their school. A six-foot wooden fence surrounded it, and it had a large dirt yard to run around.

As I got my gear ready to film, a soccer ball bounced off my shoe. A barefoot nine-year-old with the warmest smile I've ever seen was giggling at me, trying to get me to play. Before I had a chance, there was another ball. And another. And another. The volunteers had brought fifty deflated soccer balls with them, and they found themselves getting quite the workout using hand-pumps to fill them with air as fast as they could. I thought a couple of them might pass out...January in Haiti is still pretty warm. And there at the center of all of it was Wayne. While soccer was not what you would call his strongest sport, he got in and mucked it up with the dozens of grateful children who now each had a new toy and new shoes. He was having a great time, but like most of us in that heat, he had to take a break and sit down on a bench off to the side.

When given the opportunity, most children would rather play with other kids than hang out with adults. There was one child, however, who seemed to be fixated with Wayne. He appeared younger than most of these children, maybe three-years-old, and as Wayne sat at the table, the little boy came right up to him. They seemed to stare at each other for ten seconds. Wayne then reached his hand out and said, 'Gimme five.' The little boy didn't know what it meant. So, with his other hand, he took the boy's hand and gently clapped it against his. 'Gimme five.' The boy got what it meant, and he, well, gave Wayne 'five.' 'Up high.' Wayne's hand was now six inches higher. The boy, who didn't speak a word of English, understood everything. 'Up high,' it was. 'Down low.' The boy went to slap, but Wayne pulled his hand away. 'Too slow.'

The little boy smiled. They repeated this three more times, Wayne winning once, the little boy winning twice.

With my camera on my tripod, I spent the first half of the scene looking through my viewfinder. And then, I simply had to look up and see it through my own eyes, not just a camera lens. And it was in that moment when I realized just who Wayne Elsey really was: a superhero... a living, breathing superhero. No, he might not be able to leap tall buildings in a single bound or lift a car over his head, but the compassion he has for humanity, and the desire to make the world a better place for everyone he can, is one of the most heroic things I've ever seen.

As we left the orphanage that night and we walked back up the hill to our truck, I remember stopping in the middle of the path and looking back. The children were still running around like maniacs with their soccer balls, some trying to dribble two and three at a time. It was not lost on me that it was a Friday night. I thought about what I might have done on various Friday nights in my past, from going to the movies with my folks, to imbibing a few too many in my twenties with my friends, to tucking our children into bed after a long hard week at school. And then I thought about the children that played before me. I considered how they will never know the love of a mom and dad again until they become moms and dads of their own, how this is where many of them will spend their entire childhood, and how some of them (the odds suggest) will never leave the walls that protected them at this moment. And I uncontrollably wept, unimaginably sad for all that they've endured in their young lives, and yet hopeful because the world has people like Wayne, a man who will forever be my hero." – **Dan Duffy, Co-Founder, The Half Fund**

Lyssa High is an inspiration to me and has always cheered me on, and I'm as fortunate as my father to call her a friend. Because of her spirit, I can see why she and my dad have been friends for years. Lyssa serves as another example of how we're all tied together. She started by managing a garage sale for my dad and has been in our lives ever since.

I can relate to her story about a garage sale that you'll read. My father can forget what could be the little things, such as a warning sign, when he's got his mind more focused on looking for a deal—usually for ½ of what is being asked. My dad is an excellent salesman, and he loves the challenge of figuring out how to build a business and make a profit. I think he wouldn't be a great salesman if he weren't always looking for a good deal.

It's my dad's drive, passion, and love for business, I think, that has propelled him to success with his team at Funds2Orgs Group. He loves the idea of being part of the network that assists micro-entrepreneurs in developing nations obtain inventory.

As much as my dad loves leading and developing his social enterprises, one of the greatest things that he loves doing is helping others grow theirs. Today, he's called on regularly for advice and counsel on many projects, and paying it forward is something where he finds a lot of joy. But, on the little things, sometimes he can forget the details (in the following reflection case, a warning sign). As great as my dad is—no one is perfect, which is what makes him human and helps to make him so approachable.

> "I met Wayne Elsey in Nashville, TN in 1999. I was pursuing a singing career in the country music industry. I was in-between jobs when I met Wayne, and he was getting ready to move. He often traveled for his job, so he hired me to help him with this move.
>
> He and I decided to have a garage sale for some of the items he didn't need or want anymore. He bestowed the title of 'Garage Sale Manager' to me. I do not believe that Wayne had ever had a garage sale before, based on his constant questioning of my reduced prices on his 'valuables', but I assured him that I had things priced right and that he needed to trust me!
>
> My only concern for the garage sale was his steep driveway, a VERY steep driveway. I was so concerned that I put a sign at the top of the driveway stating, 'Walk down

at your own risk!' The big day arrived, and the people came from miles around to visit Wayne Elsey's Garage Sale.

Wayne came out to see how things are going, and he asked why I put a 'Walk down at your own risk' sign at the top of the driveway? Immediately after asking that question, a woman holding a 3-month-old baby came walking down the driveway and fell backward onto her bottom! She never let go of the baby, and mom and baby were perfectly fine, but what a scare for all of us. Wayne looked at me and said, 'Well, I guess we do need that sign!' He seemed to have a deeper trust in me after that event." – **Lyssa High, Lifestyle Host on Good Day Kentucky ABC 36 WTVQ, Lexington, KY**

Although I've never met April Hardcastle-Miles personally, her kind words about my dad are lovely. As an adult and mom, I've come to realize that the stories we hear about our parents are what create the legacies they leave to us.

These are the stories that I will one day share with Aubree, Aiden and Jaxon and that we will pass down through the generations in our family beginning with our children. As a parent in a young family, I'm so pleased that my father was sweet enough to gift time at his condo for a young honeymoon couple.

Again, this is but one lovely example of how we can make an impact on the life of someone that will always be remembered.

"'Walk and talk' this is a phrase that I first heard from my high school theatre teacher. Walk and talk, let the momentum of what you are saying become a physical action; move and do not waste time. This phrase describes my friend, Wayne Elsey, in such a perfect way, and it is such a perfect thing that we met in through live theatre.

I met Wayne backstage at the Lakewood Theatre while playing Babe in Crimes of the Heart. Lakewood Theatre is a small, charming space in Old Hickory, Tennessee. Wayne lived in Old Hickory and was involved with community events. His support for our show and the tiny theatre helped so much. We could never get him on stage, but he was an absolute character. As funny as he was encouraging. Pranks for days. Good ones, too. That kind of energy is so essential in a creative environment. It is contagious, and it inspires. Wayne would be in the audience greeting people he had invited into this amazing community and introducing them to the people that had lived in Old Hickory their entire lives.

More often than not, connections would be made that would benefit both all parties. It was and still is very interesting to see Wayne do that—bring people together. Wayne is one of those amazing souls that can see beyond the words, three steps ahead of the planning, and place action within the need. Wayne Elsey is a verb and does not believe in wasting time. I saw this ability but truly understood them in April of 2006. I had just gotten married, and we did not have a lot of money for a honeymoon. Wayne offered his Orlando condo to my husband and me as a wedding present. One of the nicest things anyone has ever done for us.

While there, Wayne flew into town to take us to dinner and meet some of his friends and people in the community. We would walk into a diner and hear, 'ZAPATOS!' I can still hear Wayne's nickname shouted with excitement when he would walk through the door. He introduced us to several people. Some were just casual chats, while other people needed advice about painting and construction, my husband's profession, or guidance for the best ways to get an agent, or film school projects. My husband and I were able to help a few people. Wayne makes these introductions, and people connect. Happy accidents or careful planning? I am not certain. What I do know for sure: Wayne is a human being that wants to help everyone. No one is a stranger. I feel very fortunate to have him as my friend; leading by example…walking and talking." – **April Hardcastle-Miles**

When I was young, I remember a lot of the energy that happened around the creation of Soles4Souls. Something that has come up for me in reading each of these stories and reflections, including Stacy Case's, is how one person can indeed be the change for someone else or many others.

When I was growing up, Soles4Souls played a big part in our family life, and I'm not sure that people understand that. As much as the world was looking at what my father was doing for others who had experienced humanitarian disasters or poverty, my dad was talking about stories regarding what he had seen or experienced. I think it's fair to say that a lot of the time he spent playing with children in developing countries or coordinating international deliveries of thousands of shoes to people in desperate need after a natural disaster is something that he will never forget. As much as others remember him and what he's done, all of the experiences he had at Soles4Souls and also at Funds2Orgs very much remain a part of who he is as a person.

> "I first had the honor of meeting Wayne Elsey a decade ago when I showed up to do a story on his nonprofit Soles-4Souls. It was the fastest growing charity in the world, and I wanted to see what all the fuss was about, at the time. I was immediately inspired when Wayne began describing how the idea for Soles4Souls came to him. His schedule was jam-packed as the CEO of several shoe companies globally, but news footage of the 2004 tsunami stopped him in his tracks.

> Wayne described during our interview how a single shoe floated up in the news coverage, and he knew he had to harvest all of his connections in the shoe biz to help these people. Wayne started a grassroots campaign by phone and email to get shoe donations, initially asking for a couple thousand. He ended up with a quarter million. That's how Soles4Souls was born, and Wayne has gone on to found other for-profit and not-for-profit ventures.

> In a nutshell, Wayne is able to take something simple and use it to create complex change. Wayne and I have been friends since that first day he granted me an interview and my life has been inspired by his ever since." – **Stacy Case, Former CBS News National Correspondent, Fox Nashville Main Anchor, Murrow & Emmy Award Winning Journalist, 26 Year News Veteran**

Ray Vause is "one of the guys" and also some-one who my dad has breakfast with every Wednesday. Every week, they enjoy a meal and a lot of conversation.

I want to write that there's a lot of wis-dom happening at the breakfast table, and while that may be true at times, it's more about laughs, sharing and teasing each other, and there's also a lot of preening on who's doing better. But, it's all in good fun.

Candidly, however, there is so much going on at that table each week that the few times I was there, I couldn't stay. I think they're "crazy old men," as I like to tease my dad. However, I know all of their hearts are in the right places, even if they're trying to outdo each other during their weekly breakfast time.

"When you first meet Wayne Elsey, you have immediate respect for him. It only takes a few minutes to realize that he is a hardworking, honest and generous person.

When I met Wayne, he was CEO of Soles4Souls, a charity he founded. He started it based on the knowl-edge that many people around the world had no shoes and that many Americans, such as my wife, have many pairs of shoes. Americans had many pairs of shoes they did not need, and many children around the world had no shoes. Wayne started Soles4Souls to allow people with too many shoes to provide shoes to people who had no shoes. Wayne was a successful businessman who was not pursuing an op-portunity but was wanting to help those truly in need.

Over the years, I have gotten to know Wayne and have learned that he is indeed a generous person. If you are trying to do good by working hard, Wayne is willing to work with you and help you out. He has helped out count-less friends in need and is very supportive of nonprofits he deems as good charities. Wayne has set up a business strictly for the benefit of helping charities that want to raise money. Of course, this business is shoe related. Wayne's company will buy the shoes that you collect for fundrais-ing, and he provides them to other countries where peo-ple are shoeless. It's another win-win business created by Wayne. Companies can get shoes donated to them, get paid for the shoes by Wayne, and people in developing countries can get shoes.

As a final note, Wayne is not only very charitable; he is also a nice guy. Wayne is also successful. He has successfully started and run businesses. Whoever said nice guys finish last has never met Wayne Elsey." – **Ray Vause, Friend of Wayne Elsey**

Priscilla Hall offers in the following words she contributed another view of my dad when he was leading Soles4Souls. In reading all of the kind words from others, I've realized that a pattern has arisen. The pattern is that when you do something, people notice. It's your choice if you want the impression that others have of you to be positive or negative. My dad always takes the high road, and he asks his team at work and family to do the same when the inevitable challenges arise.

It's easy not to do anything and then complain. My father isn't one of those people. He sees something that needs to be done, and he does it, even if he has no idea how it's going to work out in the end. For Soles4Souls, it worked very well, but not every venture has been a great success. Still, he's always learned.

"Wayne has been an inspiration to so many and is definitely a role model in how he leads his life. His passions in his career and the importance of his family both take a front seat, which is so important! Right now, people work, work, work. I was one of those career-obsessed individuals. But, Wayne's focus on helping others through his passions and being there for his family was where I wanted to be.

We were connected as I hosted events in my stores for his first organization, Soles4Souls. We connected through his mission, and it was then I found my calling to help the community while supporting my work passions. By gathering others to educate them on how they could help, it brought us together. Not only to give to those less fortunate, but also through the support of the local economy." **– Priscilla Willis, Director, Oak Hall**

My dad has done a lot of work in Haiti since his first visit after the Haitian earthquake. I know he loves the Haitian people and respects their love of family and commitment to creating a better path for themselves. It is a shame that this country, with very beautiful people, has had more than its fair share of political, economic and social strife.

Nadia Todres lives on the island nation and is an awesome person. My dad has spoken to me about Nadia often, and he likes when he has the opportunity to see her on her visits to his offices in Florida. He's shared with me the great commitment she has for Haiti and how he respects the work that she tirelessly does each day to help improve the lives of adults and children in Haiti. She wrote a beautiful book called *Rise Up: Empowering Adolescent Girls Through the Arts in Haiti*.

Nadia is an example of someone who walks the walk and who is on the front lines every day trying to help children in Haiti develop and thrive in a country where youth development opportunities can be scarce. Like my dad, Nadia is another person who believes that we're all tied together and because of it, we have to figure out ways to provide people with opportunities and hope.

"While there are so many stories to be told about Wayne Elsey, the one that comes to mind that most embody Wayne and what he stands for in life, in my humble opinion, is one that took place when I finally had a chance to meet him for the first time several years ago. It is the one that most exemplifies his moto, 'YOU Matter,' which prefaces his signature on all of his email correspondence. Wayne lives a life that entirely lives up to this statement. He makes, me—and others around him, feel vitally important. And that is not a sentence to be taken lightly. There is enormous weight in it; immense importance; deep empathy and compassion.

I witnessed this when I visited him at his office at Funds2Org several years ago. After I was dropped off outside his office building, he was apparently watching me from the window. So, while I took a few minutes to figure out if I was in the correct place, he came walking out to me and asked me how long I was going to stand there before coming inside. His sense of humor and warmth made me instantly feel at ease. Once inside, awaiting me on a table inside his office was a pile full of gifts—a collection of his books, a journal, a coffee mug, coasters and more.

He then proceeded to give me a tour of the office, taking me from desk to desk, from employee to employee, stopping in front of each person, introducing me to the person and sharing a short, most often an amusing, story about the person. Whether it was how they found one another, or how long the person had been working with Wayne and his team or something personal about the person, I could feel the most genuine and beautiful relationship between Wayne and his employees. Each employee seemed to have a genuinely good relationship with Wayne and felt so good around him. No one was tense or ill at ease, but instead, there was a sense of family and comradery. When it was time for the staff to come together for a meeting, Wayne remained quiet for most of the meeting. He later explained to me that he doesn't care to speak in his meetings, but instead prefers to allow his staff to talk and share amongst themselves. Wayne wants them to take the lead and feel a sense of importance and leadership. He said it was only in being quiet that he could listen and hear what they had to say.

I recall coming back to Haiti, following that visit, and wanting to implement some of the practice I had witnessed in Wayne, both in my personal life and in the work that I do with girls here in Haiti. I recall feeling that I had met an absolutely extraordinary person; one who's kindest and generosity left me moved beyond words. I wanted it to rub off on others instantly…so that my actions and words could leave others how I saw Wayne made the people around him feel.

Following this visit, and even before this visit, Wayne's actions have consistently been full of kindness and generosity. Whether it was purchasing a case of our book 'Rising Up' when it was published, so that he could give them to 30 of his friends, or his contributions on Giving Tuesday or his support of my co-founder's family, when he was murdered here in Haiti several years ago, he's always been supportive.

One gesture after another moves me. It pushes me to the point that I feel I am a different person in life, because of Wayne. I give more. I give more freely. I give because I know that I can change a life by my giving. And I know that I can warm another heart by my smile, by my words and with my actions. And if that is not the power of one person, then I don't know what is. It is as if all else does not matter—achievements, business, work—but rather the essence of who we choose to be in the world and how we choose to make others feel. That is life's ultimate purpose. I am deeply grateful to Wayne for the gift of the lessons he has shared me with and all that he has taught me."
– **Nadia Todres, Photographer, Founder Center for the Arts, Port-au-Prince, Haiti**

Concerning what Julie Hall, I'm not surprised by her words, because this is the man I see. She's been a long-time friend of my father's and demonstrates again that when we take the time to recognize that another person matters, we're remembered with warmth and kindness.

My dad is a person who is always putting others ahead of himself. That's just who he is and is something that he has ingrained in my life. I too put my family first.

During one of the times that my dad and I were discussing the book, he shared his thoughts about Julie's daughter, Katherine, and the story you'll read below about how he gave a free extended stay to this particular family. Even I had no idea about this specific story and how he had given Julie and her family this generous gift so that Katherine could obtain her therapy and the family would not have to concern itself with worry about finances.

> "I am my daughter's mother. My daughter, Katherine, has cerebral palsy and is confined to a wheelchair. Our family has sacrificed to allow her to get therapy, equipment, and support to enable her to have the best life possible. On one of many intensive therapy stints to Florida, we met Wayne Elsey, and we were warmed by his general caring and desire to help. My husband and I first noticed Wayne at the apartment pool as he would visit with all the residents and seemed to enjoy each conversation genuinely.

Our trips to Florida to get the intensive therapy our daughter needed was costly and without us even asking, Wayne expressed a desire to help. After Katherine's 6-week treatment was over, we returned to our home in Dallas, but we stayed in touch with Wayne. When we started to plan our next therapy trip, Wayne helped. He arranged for a furnished condominium for our lodging, and he would not let us pay for the months that we were staying in Florida. He really DID help. It was a huge financial relief for our family as we continued to do for our daughter beyond our means.

But that's just who Wayne Elsey is; he is a genuinely caring soul. *Tied Together: A Pathway to Hope* is a book of connections and relationships, where we may not even realize how we are connected. It is about the human race that is a matrix of relationships. We see people every day that we don't know, but our souls are connected just because we are human. Why do some connections cause such harm to others, whereas in other relationships find comfort and love? Wayne's book opened my ideas of how everybody REALLY is connected. Our souls are 'tied together.' We ALL just have to help, and for me, it started with Wayne helping my daughter.

Wayne has written many books imparting his vast knowledge on the subject of nonprofits and how to best help others. *Tied Together: A Pathway to Hope* has it all— Wayne's heart, expertise and years of experience shared with you on every page. *Tied Together: A Pathway to Hope* will warm your heart during a time when our nation needs a book like this now more than ever!" – **Julie Hall, RN, and Long-time Friend**

One time I noticed that my dad was getting a lot of messages on social media from Dana Nelson, whose reflection is the next one you'll be reading in this book. With my dad, you can't be surprised if something catches his attention and then next thing you know, you're having a conversation or tweeting at each other. That's just who he is. When his attention is caught, he gives whatever he's doing or whomever he's talking to his full attention.

Not too soon after the back and forth with Dana, I noticed pictures of Dana and my dad at conferences. How did that happen when they hadn't even known each other before they connected on social media? That's who my dad is. If he connects with you, even on social media, don't be surprised if you and he end up meeting up sooner rather than later. If you're in business, especially, and reach out to my dad, don't be surprised if he responds to you and seeks to meet you in person. He's all about the human connection, and yes, he personally monitors his social media platforms. He's never too busy, as crazy busy as he does get, to make a connection with someone. He's all about people, and they give him enormous energy. He loves people.

"I first met Wayne on Twitter. I was reading his book *Almost Isn't Good Enough*, and tweeted out several lines from the book, tagging him in the tweets without really expecting him to write back. He replied and told me that he appreciated my tweets!

After that first interaction, we adopted a relationship in which I continued to retweet him, and he continued to show his appreciation for my engagement. Since then, I have worked with Wayne on several projects, and the thing that strikes me most about him is that he consistently and truly does appreciate the people in his life. More importantly, he genuinely tells them that they are appreciated, that they have value, and that he truly cares.

Over the years, Wayne has shown his appreciation for me by connecting me to numerous people and providing opportunities to help me grow. It's in his nature to lift others and to help others develop. He believes in people, and he believes in connecting people in meaningful ways that not only help the individuals but the community as a whole.

He believes in taking opportunities and giving chances. Most importantly, he believes in building others up. He has told me more than once 'YOU Matter,' and those two simple words made me smile, made me believe in myself, and made me want to help other people believe that they matter.

Wayne has a way of connecting with people and making beneficial relationships that makes all those around him benefit from his presence. He radiates compassion to everyone he meets and brings out the best in people. I regularly recommend him and his books to others because I believe in his hope for a better world." – **Dana M. Nelson, Digital Strategist, Roundpeg**

I can't tell you how many times I have heard from my dad about how he went to the same school as I did and during his time there, he was a ladies' man. I guess he considers himself a Romeo. It's funny how I do not see any words about his romantic gestures from his high school friends. Maybe being the kind-hearted dork that he was is the same as being a great ladies' man in my dad's mind. One of the funny things about my dad is that when I was in school, he would tell me to read the notes that remain on the lockers, which all mentioned his "hotness." Nothing better than his daughter to affectionally burst his ladies' man bubble.

Nona Uecker Green is someone with whom my dad goes back a long time—to high school. But, unlike my dad likes to believe, she doesn't remember him as a ladies' man. In fact, there's not a single word about it in her reflection. Instead, she speaks to who my father is as a real person, not the fantasy he sometimes has in his mind. I'm so grateful to read what she has to say, and what she wrote about not looking away resonates with me.

Sometimes, when people are going through painful experiences, it's tempting to look away. My dad and the people who are in his life who try to live by his example try not to look elsewhere. It's important to bear witness because it's the only way to be part of the solution, even if you're just there to lend a shoulder to cry on for a friend. So many people think that unless you  make a grand gesture, it's not meaningful, but that's not true. As my dad often says, all you have to do is show up—that's it. Be present and share in an experience and when you can, try to help.

> "How many times have you looked at a homeless person asking for a hand out as you pass them by in the street with surprise and, yes, contempt? It happens as a knee jerk reaction. Your mind was intent on your business at hand, what you needed to do, where you needed to go, and here is an unexpected interruption. An unpleasant reminder that not everyone has the life you take for granted, so you divert your eyes, walk quickly away and mumble something about not having any cash. You try to forget them as fast as you can and go on with what important business you think you have.
>
> I remember doing just that many times in my life. As I've gotten older and have had many 'reality checks,' I realize that I've been close to being that homeless person several times. That desperate, beaten down person. I can say I remember vividly several encounters with 'almost me's.' I'm ashamed about a few of my reactions, my callousness at the time. Life can have a way of teaching you lessons, and if you're lucky, you listen and learn.

Here is a book was written by a man that learned early. He didn't divert his eyes. He looked and still looks for ways to make an impact. Make a difference. It may help a man or woman on the streets here in the U.S. or someone far from home, but does it really matter if they are far or near? People need others to help. Help them help themselves to lift themselves out of the bad situations they find themselves in. Self-inflicted or inflicted upon them?

Again, does it matter when they are working to change and just need a leg up to get themselves on their way? Wayne has worked most of his adult life in finding ways to do just that. He knew something early in life that took me a lot longer to grasp. Life rarely leaves anyone untouched by some kind of hardship, but one person or one small group of people can make a difference in another's life. The thing is when you help one person out, you help many others you had no idea would be affected. Wayne's work has a ripple effect. He helps out one group of persons, they help others and so on. Just think about it as you read. You can make a difference daily in someone's life no matter how small and it will multiply. Trust that 'YOU Matter.'"
– Nona Uecker Green, RN, BSN, Psychiatric Nurse, VA Hospital Omaha, Nebraska

I found it wonderful to read from Keith Greiveldinger that just by reading my dad's first published book *Almost Isn't Good Enough* he was inspired to get out there and do something. He's correct when he writes that you don't have to be a big career person.

You just have to have the motivation and spirit to get out there and do something for someone else. My dad and Keith are right; we can all get off the couch. There's always some way we can help someone else. Our lives aim to not only talk about being a positive and good person, especially toward others but get out there and do it in whatever way we can for other people.

"Wayne Elsey is a tremendous businessman, philanthropist, inspiration, but more importantly, I am honored to call him a friend. I first met Wayne at an event in New York City working in the footwear industry when he was promoting his first book *Almost Isn't Good Enough*. In the book, he described how a single image of a shoe washing ashore on a beach prompted him to get off the couch and start making a difference in peoples' lives around the world.

Up until that point, I had so much enthusiasm and energy to make a difference for others and the world, but I had no idea where to start. Much of my time and energy was dedicated to the footwear world and the people I met there. However, after meeting Wayne and reading his book, I understood more than ever the phrase, 'You make a living by what you get, but you make a life by what you give.'

Wayne inspired me that very day. Even though I was not a doctor, lawyer, or philanthropist, I could make a difference in others' lives and the world. I could use the platform I was in as he showed me. Someone in the foot-wear world can make a tremendous impact on others. After reading his book and meeting, Wayne inspired me to step out of my comfort zone to help others, and it forever changed my life.

I started creating videos the very next day on pro-moting positivity and inspiring others to reach higher in life and win the day. If it were not for Wayne and his story of being moved by a single shoe, I would have waited and waited to make a difference in the world. Wayne taught me the importance of stepping out and doing something that may require you to step out of your comfort zone and that there is no perfect time other than the present to do that. I also discovered that when helping others, and it is truly the greatest gift you can give and receive.

I never personally witnessed a moment like Wayne and the shoe washing ashore. However, meeting Wayne was my life-changing moment.

Years later I was living in Orlando, FL. and follow-ing Wayne on social media and noticed he posted about his big move to Orlando. I knew this was my opportunity to connect further with someone I was following and learn-ing from afar. I reached out to Wayne and welcomed him to Florida and eagerly invited him to meet over a cup of coffee. He soon accepted, and I could not understand why he would want to meet with someone like me that was not a prominent executive or someone making big waves in the business or even footwear world at that time. However, when I finally met with Wayne, he provided me a fundamental lesson and principle that I matter and everyone we meet matters!

From that moment on, I had the inspiration and the confidence to make a difference in the world as Wayne inspired me to make a social impact. He also taught me that a person matters and can make a difference with something as simple as spreading a positive message to others in need. Those in need are all of us that merely need to be reminded that the world is full of amazing and positive people; we just need to take the time to meet them and listen to them. My life changed first when I read Wayne's book, but then when I met him, he became even more of an inspiration to be a change agent for positivity in the world.

I encourage you not only to read this book but get off your couch and make a difference in those around you and the world. I can't thank Wayne enough for his inspiration, mentorship, but more importantly the change he inspired in me and millions around the world to make a difference." – **Keith Greiveldinger, Change Agent, Win it Minute Productions, Sales Manager-Rockport Company**

I met Matt Freimuth at a few BB&T events with my dad. He and Matt would joke that they first met on April 1, 2012, which is the day that Matt became my dad's personal banker. Imagine that; imagine having your banker as your friend. Perhaps in the old days, decades ago, that was something that happened, but not anymore, especially as we do so much online. But, my dad firmly believes that no matter who you are, you're a human being and life is so much better getting to know each other.

On their 5th anniversary, Matt bought my dad a wooden watch, and my dad sent a dozen roses to Matt's office, which is very funny. It is one of those stories I'm sure I'll be sharing with my kids someday in the future. Ultimately, about those beautiful roses, I know it was Matt's wife who became the beneficiary of the roses she received from "Matt." I hope I didn't reveal a secret there, but it goes to show what a kid-at-heart my dad can be in his life. Who sends roses to their banker?

"Wayne Elsey has been a good friend, business acquaintance, and mentor of mine for many years. I reflect upon the time when I was first introduced to Wayne, commencing my career in banking simultaneously as Wayne was founding Funds2Orgs, April 1st, 2012. The date still resonates strongly with us as we jovially consider it our 'anniversary.' It was the date our business relationship officially commenced, which has since developed into a lifelong bond.

Upon hearing of the news that the successful leader from Soles4Souls was relocating to Orlando, Florida, to commence his new venture I was excited about the opportunity to secure my first client relationship in the professional world. Wayne, being a highly motivated and driven individual, was looking for his new banking partner to keep up with his fast pace and desire to succeed. From our first meeting, I could tell that whatever Wayne set out to accomplish was destined to prosper.

Wayne possesses a unique combination of business intellect, leadership, and passion that makes the world a better place. Most importantly, Wayne understands the value of relationships in all aspects of his life, and he truly cares about people. When you have a good value system and focus on building relationships, you will yield positive results in both  your business and personal life." – **Matthew Freimuth, Vice President, Regional Corporate Banking, BB&T**

I can relate to the words as written by Caroline Farley. My dad would embarrass me talking to everyone, as he knows a lot of people. My dad loves to rib and tease people, and the more you get to know him, the more you realize that's just who he is—usually looking for a good laugh.

I will never forget the time we are in Disney World, and with 80,000 people in the park, we stopped and talked to two couples he knew and worked with in prior years. Yes, my dad loves to talk and tease people, es-

pecially me as a kid, and in a park with 80,000 people, he can meet people he knows, strikes up conversations and then tells these people silly little things about me.

To make things more fun, he also tried to strike up conversations with random strangers. All I wanted to do was to get on the rides— which he was afraid of doing. So, talking to people became the diversionary tactic of choice!

"'YOU Matter,' the two words that initiated a significant life pivot for me. Two simple words that continually challenges me to not only make the best out of every situation but to be the best human I can be during my time on Earth. These two words first came through to me in an email from Wayne back in 2012.

I was young, and I was working in media sales as my first job out of college. I had just finished my degree in Nonprofit Leadership and decided to take an associate publisher role for a fundraising publication hoping to make a difference in the nonprofit community by creating a community of innovators and educators. I inherited a book of business from my predecessor, and Funds2Orgs was one of those accounts that had not been called. I did my research and was intrigued by their model, an innovative and unique approach to helping nonprofits fundraise while providing support to local business owners in developing countries. I started to dig deeper and read up on the CEO, Wayne Elsey, and was instantly taken aback by his plethora of success with a portfolio of companies.

My first thought was, this entrepreneur has no time for me, but it was worth a try. I emailed Wayne to introduce myself not expecting anything back, as that was the norm in my line of work. But to my surprise, I received an email within 5 minutes asking me to call him and right below his note was his signature with 'YOU Matter.' That email not only began years of a business partnership but mentorship and friendship.

Before I called Wayne, I sat back in my chair and thought about the two words, 'YOU Matter.' How could two words and one email be such an inspiration and spark an entirely new attitude and passion for my job? I picked up the phone and called Wayne and was greeted with a, 'Hey, pal.' How could such a successful individual have so much warmth and genuine respect for me, just another salesperson calling? Well, it soon became apparent. Wayne functions at an entirely different level than most people I know. His values, passion, and positivity are contagious. You can feel it when he speaks and how he engages with his colleagues and peers.

That one call was the beginning of many business conversations and the start of a new outlook on life. Wayne and his inspirational values guided opened my mind to a new way of thinking during a very pivotal time in life. One specific meeting with Wayne completely solidified my initial thoughts on who he was as a person and entrepreneur.

A few months after our call and the start of our business partnership, I planned my first sales trips to Orlando to meet with clients. I spent weeks planning and calling on prospects to set meetings with many ignored emails. But when I called Wayne to ask for a meeting, he not only immediately invited me to his office but also insisted I join him and Courtney at their home for a homecooked meal.

It may sound like a small gesture to most, but to me, it was another pivotal moment that humanized my job. We spent the evening speaking about what is truly important in life. What I valued and what was important to me personally and professionally. When we met at his office, I had a moment of clarity when I saw how Wayne engaged with his colleagues as peers. He was not the boss, but an equal contributor, supporting his team in every way possible. Another incredible testament to Wayne and his success was when he shared with me that he doesn't hire based on a fancy resume, but rather looks to bring on individuals who can make an impact regardless of their history, giving chances to individuals who might not be given an opportunity at a career with a large corporation. That fact alone encourages entrepreneurship and social good.

In a day where business deals are simply done over emails, and in a series of negotiations where sales reps flexed their muscles to close deals, Wayne taught me that trust, friendship, and humanization is the real key to success. Success is also defined in many different ways and unique to each individual. But overall, success is true happiness in all aspects of your life. Find work that feeds your soul and never do anything that compromises your values.

Shortly after that dinner, I left my company to take a more rewarding opportunity where I could own something, be true to my values and fulfill myself personally. Wayne's beliefs are ones I have continued to embrace and carry not only professionally but personally—how one individual—and even a straightforward interaction between two people can make a difference of a lifetime. A smile, a nice gesture, answering a call and simply just treating every single person with respect can make one person feel they matter because they do.

From the very beginning, Wayne showed me how authenticity and humanity is the core to making an impact. It doesn't take millions of dollars nor having a national platform to impact lives. Each person on this earth is a living breathing human and can make a positive impact on another, and this small impact can soon turn into a more substantial impact with a domino effect. A big house, fancy cars, large bank accounts or hefty expense account do not make me any different from a stranger on the bus or a child in a developing country like Haiti.

To this day, I still call Wayne with new ideas and even though months and years may pass, he always answers with a 'Hey, pal,' as no time has passed. This past week, our paths crossed again as one of Wayne's companies will be supporting the company my team, and I have worked three years to build. I cannot be more grateful to have his support and work together to make a few more ripples of good on Earth.

I do not have all the secrets to life nor am I anywhere near perfect, no one is, even Wayne (but he sure is closer than I am!). But we are humans and continue to support one another to enrich our own lives and those around us. No matter what challenges or interactions lie ahead, I hope this book and Wayne's stories show you that anything is achievable, as he has for me. 'YOU Matter' along with everyone in this world. I hope my story and all the others encourage you to make that call, take a chance, look at any silver lining or simply talk to others like they are human because they are. They matter and most importantly, 'YOU Matter.'" – **Caroline Farley, Chief Growth Officer, Shoptalk & Groceryshop**

When I read Jorelle Nowlin's comments below, I asked my dad about it, and he said he didn't remember. Even if he does remember doing something good for someone else, he's humble. Despite the towering personali-

ty that he has, he's a humble person, and he doesn't like to toot his own horn.

I really think he does remember, but he always tries to keep a distance from his good works as they are natural or second nature to him. He doesn't want to be anyone's hero. He's just looking to do the right thing by people.

"As kids, Wayne and I were neighbors in a rural part of Virginia where Wayne and my brother attended the same school. There was an incident that my brother had with some boys attended the same school, which made my brother fearful of returning to school. Wayne soon came to discover what had happened and that my brother was refusing to go to school. So, Wayne chose to reach out to him and headed down to my house. He reassured my brother that no harm would come to him, and he should return to school because Wayne would be looking out for him. With Wayne's, help not only did my brother return to school,

but my brother was able to identify the boys responsible and turn them in. It was nearly 30 years later that I was seeing a guy, Wayne Elsey, on television and hearing about the inspirational journey and success of Soles4Souls not realizing that this was the same Wayne that had been there for my brother. It is touching to realize that young boy took that kind compassionate heart and grew into a man who used those qualities to change the lives of so many, as though he was born to make a difference in the world. Truly inspirational." – **Jorelle Nowlin**

When I read Chris Brayton's comments, the first thoughts that came to me were that I think what she was trying to say was that my dad had a lot of energy—and he was a pain in the rear, bugging her for extra marketing materials to help his stores performance.

The reality is that my dad is an impatient businessman, but that's because he believes that there is so much to be done. You couldn't possibly do what he's accomplished in his life with his team of people and not be restless. If you know my dad, then you understand that his mind is always working. Even when he's relaxing on the beach in his beloved place, there's always energy. I suppose that he's a person who could be considered a force of nature and is someone who is continually looking for opportunities for himself and others.

The fact that Chris still took the time to send something in support of my dad demonstrates the warm feelings between them. Even if you're a pain or demanding, if it's for making things better, that's the right thing to do. You'll never be forgotten.

"Back in the early to mid-80s, I lived in Boston and worked for Stride Rite Retail Corp. I was the marketing/advertising manager for 150+ stores spread all over the country. My name was Chris Kirby back then.

One day, my phone started ringing and when I answered, this bright, cheerful, energetic voice introduced himself to me as Wayne Elsey. He had just joined the company, as I believe, as the assistant manager at one of the locations in Washington, D.C. He was full of ideas and very excited to be on board and wanted to increase sales tremendously. His major thing was special promotions getting people into the store so he wanted support from me in the form of giveaways any kind of promotional items that I could come up with to create.

This young man kept me busy. Out of all of the locations, he was the only one that I could expect a phone call from at least weekly with another idea. If I hadn't liked him so much, I would've probably called him a pest. LOL

I knew from those early days that he was special and that he would go far in the world. It wasn't long before he became the manager and then a district manager and everywhere he went, he was successful. I will always consider Wayne a dear friend. It was impossible to say no to Wayne when he had one of his ideas because he was so full of energy, so bubbly, so excited—you just wanted to do whatever it took to help him pull off his ideas.

My name is now Chris Brayton. I am living in Georgia, and I'm happily retired. I consider Wayne a dear friend and enjoy keeping up with his incredible continued success. Doesn't surprise me a bit that he is where he is now because that's the kind of young man he was too." – **Chris Brayton**

Bill Reese is a great guy. My dad told me how Bill had put the car he bought for me in the warehouse and put a big bow on it for my birthday. Every time I would go to the car warehouse, I looked for my car, which my dad got for me when I was 13—as opposed to 16. But don't worry, I wasn't driving it.

The reason my dad bought me a car three years earlier than he was supposed to do it was because he wanted to be cool—although he won't admit it. Buying me a car was the excuse he needed to drive a hot car for three years and get it prepared for me.

I was just the ready excuse, which was not fair (smile) because he

got the car and I didn't for some years. When I finally got the car, however, I told my dad he needed to step up his game and give me a bow on the car. Maybe next year when I'm 30, I'll get a new car (um…Lexus would be nice—subtle hint), with a bow.

"I met Wayne through a friend of mine over 15 years ago. Over the years Wayne has helped me through some difficult times in my businesses, never asking for a thing, only wanting to help. I have learned so much from him and to this day if I have any issues, work or personal, he is always there for me. His love to help people is undeniable. You can see it through the work he has done over the last 14 years building organizations that are making a difference in this world. Good luck with the book!" – **Bill Reese, President, Eagle Apparel Sourcing And Printing**

Vickie Clark-Jennings went to high school with my dad. I have to be frank that when I was reading the words she wrote, she saw a part of him in her reflection about my father, that I've never seen.

Come on, Vickie—my dad has never been quiet…were you talking about someone else? Lol.

"Wayne and I went to high school together, which makes our age then seem like a lifetime ago. In high school, to me, Wayne seemed quiet, shy and was never one to stir the pot. I saw him around the school, but I never really got to know him. We reconnected years later while I lived in Las Vegas. He was in town, and we grabbed dinner, and that was all it took. Today, he is my admired friend, for sure. I see my friend as a man that has decided to contribute to a world in need of contribution; a man that has a message, a message that is filled with power and greatness, should we choose to be a part of it. This book will encourage and enlighten you, and more importantly, share with you that you have the power to participate in change. A change that reignites your inner light and re-establishes a belief that we are all created with the greatness to make our world a better place for generations to come. Make a decision to get involved because you make a difference." – **Vickie Clark-Jennings, Broker Associate, Berkshire Hathaway HomeServices Select Realty**

I know that there's a discussion on the pros and cons of social media, but we all know that it's not going anywhere and is how many of us communicate. Sometimes I check out my dad's timelines or posts, and it's great to see that he's got people following up, such as Bobbie Romaine, who worked with him during his early years in the footwear industry. But, he's also got many people who communicate quite regularly with him and have never had the pleasure to meet him in person. I know he's got lots of people who are great supporters of his work and motivational ideas.

I know I'm Wayne's daughter, but if you know him personally or online, you're going to get to know a person who is a straight shooter. He's also someone who finds, as I've mentioned, incredible energy from people. I know that as a young man, my dad has said of himself that he was awkward and sometimes quiet. However, he understood through the years that one of his best assets was the genuine interest that he took in people. And, he made that one of his greatest strengths.

"Many years ago, I had the pleasure of meeting Wayne Elsey while we were both employed by Stride Rite Retail Corp, Children's Shoe Division. I was an administrative assistant to the controller/financial officer, and Wayne was one of our district or regional managers. At the time, he appeared to be a go-getter with the humor and wherewithal required to lead and do an honorable job. I knew then he would go far and has no doubt exceeded all our expectations. Many of us now cheer him on via Facebook and adore his shares of family life." – **Bobbie Romaine, Long-time Friend, Stand-Besider and Cheerer-On**

Ken Wall and my dad seem to have a bromance going. I've never personally met Ken, but my dad likes him a lot and has mentioned him to me in conversations we've had. Ken is yet another example of my father's style...you can connect with him and next thing you know, you're meeting with him.

My dad loves taking chances on people and give them the opportunity to prove themselves. There are many stories of my dad connecting with people in some fashion and next thing you know, he's trusted them to execute on some aspect of his work. My dad truly is someone who likes to see a resume, but then he tosses it aside. For him, it's a person's potential and the feeling that he gets from them that matter most. If he feels the energy, passion and drive to do big things, he's someone who's happy to become their supporter or champion, and when he can, he invites them into his crazy world where the "impossible" is made "possible"—regularly. Don't tell my dad and his team that they can't do something. They'll set out to prove you wrong and have fun while they're doing it.

> "I remember the first contact I had with Wayne. He reached out to me asking what services I offered and for pricing. I remember clicking on his name in the Facebook chat window and saw that he has a 'Blue Checkmark' next to his name on his PERSONAL profile page! I was like...'Whoa! This dude is definitely somebody!' You don't get a blue checkmark unless you've done some great things!
>
> Fast forward to me flying to Orlando to officially meet Wayne and talk business. I'll never forget it! He comes walking out in jeans and loafers, and I believe a golf shirt! He then decided to take me to lunch. I can recall thinking, 'WOW! The CEO of this big successful organization (who has a blue checkmark) is taking me to lunch! This is gonna be a serious 5-star experience!'
>
> So, I followed him to the restaurant. When we parked in the parking lot of the plaza, I began scanning the area looking for what could be a 5-star restaurant. It wasn't the worst part of town, but it did not appear we were in any 'upscale' area.
>
> So, he pops out of his car and motions for me to follow him. He began walking toward some Italian restaurant that looked like a tiny little hole-in-the-wall joint! I followed him into the place. It was a small hole-in-the-wall! I was really surprised that 'Mr. Blue Checkmark' would ever want to eat at such a place! LOL. But, I quickly realized that this place was a secret; not to mention that he knew the owners (like they were family to him)! It turned out to be the very

best meatball sandwiches that I had ever had. Wayne treated everyone in that place like family, and they reciprocated. I imagine that most people feel this way about Wayne after spending 5 minutes with him.

If I were to guess what the number one factor related to Wayne's success and happiness in life is, I would say it is the fact that he genuinely does care about every single person he meets. I've never been in his presence or hung up from a phone conversation with him without feeling better about myself. The guy just has that magic touch that many people do not possess. He always makes others feel good about themselves. There is the saying, 'People will often forget what you said to them, but they will ALWAYS remember how you made them feel.' Wayne is a walking example of this. Honored and grateful to call him a friend!" – **Ken Walls, CEO, Client Solution Innovations**

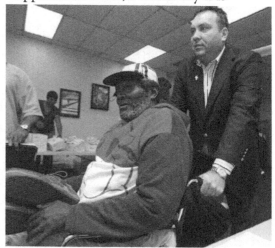

Teri Griege is someone for whom my dad has a tremendous amount of respect, admiration, and affection for in his life. He believes that she's a rock star and he will always do anything to share her story with others.

Teri is another cancer survivor, and she is terrific, and so is her organization, Powered by Hope, which sums up her awesome fight against cancer. Like my dad, Teri is the type of person who will never give up, no matter the challenge, and Teri is very much a kindred spirit. I understand why he considers her a close friend. Teri is also an author and wrote, *Powered By Hope: The Teri Griege Story*, which is another book, as is Dan Duffy's that can be of great inspiration for someone dealing with cancer.

"What I first knew about Wayne, was that he was helping people by finding shoes and donating them. Then I learned how his life was changed when he turned on the TV and saw a shoe washing up on the beach after the tsunami hit Indonesia. Wayne then took the time to educate me on micro-businesses. He patiently explained how he was changing the lives of the people of Haiti, one shoe at a time. When I saw his passion for helping people and how he used his knowledge of the shoe industry to help others, it gave me the confidence to do the same. I am full of gratitude for

being taught this valuable lesson. Wayne talks about 'hope.' For me, HOPE means Helping Other People Every Day. That idea describes Wayne." – **Teri Griege, Founder & President, Powered by Hope**

Jeff Goodnough's thoughts about my father are very true. He's a person who is continually challenging his team because he's restless and that helps propel the people who work with him to reach greater heights. I should know because when I've worked with him, he's been relentless in pushing me to do better.

As I've said of my dad, there's always a new idea brewing. Sometimes I view my dad as an orchestra conductor, and he has the strings, brass, percussion, and woodwinds in front of him, about to be the maestro at a performance. When he walks into the office and even when he's on the road, he's the conductor making sure that everyone is hitting the right notes, and what happens is full of sound, life, activity, and energy.

"1998-1999 I had the pleasure of working with Wayne at Iron Age Safety Shoes. At the time I was a MM/DSM for 3 locations of Iron Age and Knapp shoes in Eastern Michigan. If I remember correctly, Wayne had recently started with the company and came to work with me as my VP.

My situation with the company was that I moved and worked in several different states and locations, moving up through the proverbial ranks (my father was an old shoe dog and VP of Ops in NY). I had wanted to move back East because I had done all the traveling and started a new family. I was turned down for a position that I was overqualified for but would bring me back east. I think

I had met Wayne maybe twice when I provided him my resignation. I was in a very rough place—first career job, proven success, new family, new house, need to get closer to home—and with a sincere appreciation and instant connection with Wayne! I remember the first introduction and phone calls with Wayne. He was asking questions, challenging me, having high expectations, telling me about his home and the lake (spending time with his daughter, boating), showing interest in my family, in general, it was a great feeling to look forward working together.

We had lunch in a local student hangout restaurant near the University of Michigan. I was nervous, anxious, conflicted, and could feel it in my presence. I probably stuttered, 'I'm going to be providing my notice...' The complete opposite of what I expected happened. I saw a huge Wayne Elsey smile. His hand extended in congratulations, and he said, 'Tell me about this exciting news!' Wayne went on to share that he was so happy for me and made me not to feel all those gut-wrenching feelings because I was doing the right thing. 'Do what's right for you and your family and stay in touch,' he said. I think from the introduction to that point I knew Wayne only a couple of months. However, from that point, each time we've connected over the years has produced the same feelings. I have always been extremely motivated anytime I read about new happenings or simple posts by Wayne. It's silly because I also remember that time was before smartphones and WiFi. We had phone booths spotty cell phones, dial-up, and the only social media was a gathering with people! I'm very proud to know Wayne and love knowing 'I matter!'" – **Jeff Goodnough, Glass Apps General Manager Plant Production and Client Management**

Sometimes life can connect people in strange ways, and Linda Spencer's story is an example of that idea. Her mom was raised in poverty, and the idea of shoes is what eventually captured Linda's attention about my dad when she wrote about him for her blog many years later. And, like often happens, once she entered into my dad's orbit, she became a part of it on his team.

"My mother was raised in poverty in Colombia. Her family

was poor, and because of it, my mother suffered a lot growing up and had limited opportunities. One of the things I remember my mother talking about as I grew up was how her family could not afford shoes for her, which meant she could not attend school.

Flash forward decades. My mother raised two daughters in the U.S., including me. Once I was done with my fundraiser career, I decided to explore my life as a writer. At the time, I created a blog and had only been writing a month. I always wanted to write and was an English major in college. I happened on an article about Wayne who had been in the shoe business but decided to serve as a bridge between people living in poverty and in need of shoes. I was intrigued, and the story captured my imagination, particularly because my mom was one of the people who could have used good shoes when she was growing up. I wrote a post about him on my now defunct blog.

Next thing you know, he tweeted me, and I was flown from New York to Florida. Within weeks I was working for his brands writing. Up to that point, I had been a professional fundraiser, but Wayne gave me a shot following my passion for writing. Why? Just because. But, that's Wayne. He's willing to give people a chance. I've been writing for his brands ever since. It's been five years.

Within four months of starting with Wayne and his team, I moved to Europe with my husband, which was a significant life change. Admittedly, I thought I would lose my opportunity with a group of people I enjoyed. I couldn't have been more incorrect. Wayne kept me on the team and did everything to make sure I always felt 'connected,' which turned out to be very important because I had to acclimate as an American to European life, with different cultures and lives. I've since learned that you can take the New Yorker and American out of that great city and big country, but you can't take away the filter through which many expats, including me, view their adopted places to live.

What I like so much about Wayne are his vision, energy and incredible spirit. He reminds me very much of both my dad and my husband. My dad was a man who also knew no limits. Zero. Wayne is very much the same way.

My husband believes nothing is impossible. He's another one who drank that Kool-Aid. I find that 'can do' spirit, vision, determination and boundless energy to be something that is so motivating and inspirational for me and I'm fortunate to count Wayne among the handful of people who have been significant parts of my life.

Wayne's crafted a team of equals in his office and every week I look forward to connecting with 'my team'—from Europe. It takes quite an emotionally intelligent person to create a work environment where someone 4,428 miles and 6 hours ahead in time can always feel part of the team.

This is a once in a lifetime experience for me, and I thank everyone in our group. Together, with Wayne's vision and leadership, we are building something—a legacy which flows with impact—in multiple social enterprises and other businesses. Every day is a master class entrepreneurship,  learning—and being a better person!" – **Linda N. Spencer, Content Creator, Elsey Enterprises**

Tony DiFranco's story that follows is yet another example of the work my dad and his team have done with shoes. It's incredible—still—to think that a pair of shoes can become the currency and in the case of Tony and his group, the shoes helped fund the needs of an organization serving 80,000 people in Africa.

One of the things that many people and I admire of the work my dad does with his team is that they've figured out an excellent solution for helping so many. Often, especially now with some of my children in school, there's a request for money for additional programs, events or experiences that are not funded by grants. Selling candy, I think it's fair to say, is not the highlight to a parent's involvement in fundraising, but collecting shoes is really brilliant.

I'm proud of the fact that my dad figured out how to help people with shoes, and then he created Funds2Orgs Group and not only helped micro-entrepreneurs around the world but also schools, groups, and so many others in their fundraising.

"I met Wayne Elsey soon after I had fully immersed myself into the nonprofit sector. I was surprised that Wayne's interest in me was not based on my experience and passion but was based on who I was as a person. His focus was set on how he could bring value to me, and in doing so, give me the inspiration and practical tools so that I could bring value to the world around me. Since our first conversation, Wayne has become an invaluable resource, a trusted advisor, and an encouraging friend.

Opening a medical clinic in Burundi, Africa is no small task. Fortunately, I am not the person who has to construct the building or train the medical staff. As a member of the board of directors for The Cries of a Child, my role is in governance, and of course, fundraising. The latter is not my strength. After several years of praying, planning, and persevering, we were getting close to being able to open a facility that would serve 80,000 people in one of the most desperate lands on earth. We lacked the funding to complete the project. We needed equipment and furnishings.

I reached out to Wayne, who I had met a year prior. Wayne showed me how we could convert shoes—yes, shoes—into the cash for our organization. Within two months, with Wayne's guidance, we had secured the funds we needed to complete the clinic and open our doors. Two years later, the clinic has served tens of thousands of Burundians who would otherwise have limited or no access to health care." – **Tony DiFranco, NonProfit Marketing Entrepreneur and Awesomeness Innovator**

Wes Morrison is a council member from Cape Canaveral that my dad has mentioned often to me. One of my dad's favorite places is on the beach. I guess you can say it's his happy place and his home in Cape Canaveral, which he shares with Courtney and their dog, Brody, is where he finds the space to recharge.

I know that he and Courtney think Wes is a great person who is grounded, and they enjoy what he's done for them in sharing his time and the community.

"Wayne Elsey is a man who has mastered the ability to bring the best out in others. One can quickly see that his inner compass points in a direction that brings a breath of fresh air for our generation. While we may live in some of the best times in human history from a survival standpoint, we face some of the most complicated dividing cultural and social issues.

Tied Together: A Pathway to Hope gives us hope, thanks to the virtuous trailblazers like Wayne and his team. The book brings an abundance of wisdom, experience, and inspiration to overcome these difficult challenges. Wayne is an empathetic listener and an impressively competent leader while proclaiming a courageously inspiring vision for a cleaner, safer and more beautiful world. To put it simply, Wayne is a leader one would dream of having on their team and reading this book essentially makes that happen.

This timely message taps into the heart and mind of every reader by recognizing that all people desire the ability to receive and give appreciation, respect, and love. In contrast, the book also exposes the awful realities of clear division from Wayne's first-hand experiences. The reader will understand the opportunity for our generation to listen while leveraging hope in the face of fear. Suddenly, the overwhelming need and task to make a difference in the world become one that is well within our reach."
– Wes Morrison, City Council Member, Cape Canaveral, Florida

The next reflection is written by Silvana Clark who gives us another view of my dad and the way he thinks.

Yes, this is the guy whom you can call, without knowing him, and suggest that you'll drive an RV across the U.S. promoting his organization, and he'll take you up on it. How many people would do that? People could say that it's a crazy or ridiculous idea, especially because my dad didn't know Silvana at the time, but he doesn't look at the world like that. Instead, if he gets the right feeling, and he sees the potential and opportunity, no idea is too crazy or ridiculous. It takes a special kind of person to be like that in life; don't you think?

No idea is too wild for my father, and that's another reason, I think that he's been able to make things happen. His thinking is never constrained or limited, and if you want to develop your social enterprise, you should heed his words. Do it and don't bow to limited thinking. My dad and the group of people who work with him genuinely believe anything is possible and they don't worry about something not being done. If an idea has never been done before, or if it's a significant challenge, they work through the problem until they figure out how to execute it well. I don't think I've ever heard anyone who works with my dad, or my father himself, say something isn't possible. It's always possible.

"My husband and I were involved with Soles4Souls on a casual basis, by collecting shoes and supporting the company in general. We approached Wayne with the wild idea of having us travel the U.S. in an RV, promoting Soles4Souls across the country, while also distributing new shoes to people in need. Like a true leader, Wayne decided without spending months on committees and logistics. He bought an RV and gave us a call saying, 'The RV is ready. Can you be here in three weeks?' We were! We spent 19 months crisscrossing the U.S. in a branded RV, letting the country know about the great work of Soles4Souls. It was a bold idea. Wayne saw the possibilities in an unusual marketing plan and set his charity apart from the others." – **Silvana Clark, Speaker/Author/Brand Ambassador**

Timothy Rasmussen shows us, again, how believing in someone else can change a life. His story also demonstrates how my dad believes in potential. You'll see how he got someone who was renting one of his properties to write for his businesses.

When you meet someone who you think can do something, as my dad thought with Tim, just go ahead and let them do their thing. My father is not the kind of business leader that cares about fancy resumes or degrees. He's the person who cares about someone's motivation to do something. He's impressed by the potential for the future and not so much by what they've done in the past.

He could be your landlord, as he was with Tim, and the next thing you know, he's hiring you to write for him. It doesn't matter with my father. It's all about a person's connection with him, their energy and potential.

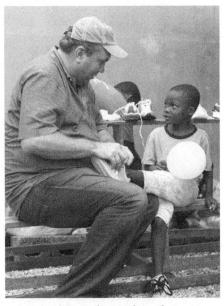

"Every Day Is Pay-Day. Pretty much every writing opportunity I've ever had has come to me organically, as in I wasn't expecting it or actively pursuing it. I certainly wasn't seeking a writing gig when I signed a lease to rent a beautiful 2-bedroom condo in a gated Orlando country club community. The gregarious property owner couldn't have been more accommodating, allowing us to move in early and even offering to put the rent towards purchasing the property if I so desired at the end of the lease. In fact, after he discovered that I took on freelance writing projects in between recording and touring gigs, he even offered me a writing project in just my initial conversation meeting him. He needed help adapting his first book into a coordinating workbook to accompany his corporate speaking engagements. It sounded promising, but my first thought was…who was my new landlord? He was Wayne Elsey.

That first project turned into another, which turned into another, and more and more. Wayne's vision for helping as many people around the world is contagious. I had never written for anything in the nonprofit sector before, but my previous involvement with charities near to my heart remain as some of my proudest professional and personal moments. The picture of who Wayne is and what makes him tick became instantly clear with every meeting, brainstorming session, phone call, text between us. Here's a typical afternoon phone call between Wayne and me during the time I worked on his projects:

Calls Wayne's cell phone and he picks up:

'Hey, Tim, what's up man? Don't I owe you some money? Come over to the house; I'll have a check for you.'

'Hey Wayne, you don't owe me anything. You paid me last week, remember? I don't have any outstanding invoices at the moment, and I will shoot you one when we finish writing this website.'

'Ok sounds great, just send it to me. Everything ok at the condo? How's the new refrigerator working? I just felt that a new one would be better than trying to fix the old one for the third time. It had given me problems before.'

'It's awesome, Wayne. I'm still kind of shocked you had it over here a day after I called you about the issue on the old one. Thank you so much.'

'Not a problem, Tim. What's up, what can I do for you?'

'I actually just wanted to run something by you. I know we talked about organizing the main page with bullet points, I was thinking maybe I could draft mini-paragraphs with supporting bullets that—'

'Oh yeah, I love it! I can see it now; I'm surprised we didn't think of that originally. Hey Tim, I'm walking out of the door as we speak. I need to meet with one of my shoe industry guys who wants to partner with us. I will be back home around 4:00 and you can call me if you need anything else. I love your idea; I trust you. Keep it up, Rock Star!'

'You got it, Wayne, have a great meeting.'

There's a ton of little nuances in just a regular, 2-minute phone conversation with Wayne that illustrates the way he brings everything together. He's aggressive in attacking his mission to help as many people as possible. He uses his connections to make the mission stronger than it would be on his own. For his team members, he trusts, empowers and values them. The fact that I was a tenant in one of his properties and a freelancer for his social enterprises, he always made sure I had everything I needed to be successful. I never had to chase him to get paid; he went out of his way to make sure I was taken care of, always. That makes me feel incredibly valued and supported. That makes me want to work harder and deliver the best writing and strategy that I can provide. It makes me feel connected. It was also an incredible feeling to know that every piece I worked on for Wayne had an actual impact on it.

If something I wrote helped inspire the next partner that furthered the cause, or even encouraged someone to donate or do something charitable on their own, somebody around the world is the beneficiary of that goodwill and empathy, that's powerful. And what's more, that has a different value than when I get up on stage and perform or release an album with my face and name on it. If somebody is inspired or moved by a song I create, I still get the shine and gratification from it. Working on projects with Wayne reminded me that humility and generosity without seeking credit is the ultimate service. This kind of work is the reward itself, not the paycheck. In fact, sometimes I really would forget to invoice Wayne, and part of that comes from already feeling compensated by the feeling I got when I was that connected to what I was working on, who I was serving.

Wayne is exactly right; we are all 'tied together.' And when you are serving others, connected by empathy for your fellow humans, then it truly feels like every day is payday." – *Timothy Rasmussen b/k/a $hamrock, Vh1/ MTV personality, national recording artist & songwriter.*

Reverend Yeargin's reflection on my dad's work is humbling. Think about it as you read it. Here, in the U.S., one of the wealthiest countries in the world, many kids have never been able to own a pair of flip-flops, which can be as cheap as $10.

But, when families are living in poverty, I can see how parents decide not to buy their kids flip-flops and make sure when they purchase footwear that it's something more practical and can be used to go to school.

"I first met Wayne on a project through the Donelson/Hermitage Chamber of Commerce. This project was one to gift flip-flops to students in the Donelson Hermitage Area during the last few weeks before the summer break. These gifts included 10 elementary schools, four middle schools and one high school. I didn't fully grasp the magnitude of this man's gift until I heard on several occasions, students state to me, 'How cool. I've never had a pair of flip-flops.'

This project pulled together area leaders, businesses, teachers, counselors—all wanting to gift some students with a little joy before beginning summer break. It all started with one man's idea of 'flip-flops.' Not only did the students benefit—we benefited as a community—pulling together to create a little hope and connection in our community. I encourage you to read *Tied Together: A Pathway to Hope.* Wayne has a big heart and has a vision that could literally change our world as we know it today. Isn't it time?" – **Rev. Denise Yeargin, Senior Minister, Unity of Music City**

My dad has been interviewed many times throughout his career and the work he does with his teams, and Keith Landry has been one of the people who've done it.

I find it incredible that journalists and media professionals, who get to see countless stories, choose to follow him when the camera has been turned off, and the segment has been recorded. That means that someone made such an impression, that despite the countless stories they report on at any time, they want to remember the one about my dad and his work to make the world a better place.

"I still remember the first time I met Wayne Elsey. I was a TV news anchor in Orlando, FL. He showed up at the station fifteen minutes early for our visit, something he has made a point to do for his appointments throughout his career.

I interviewed the founder of Soles4Souls about his mission to use nonprofit work to help some of the most impoverished and desperate people on our planet. I wondered after our interview, 'What makes a CEO like that tick, and how does he perform at such a high level to make a difference on a global basis?'

I have followed Wayne's work ever since. He has spent many years visiting nearly hopeless places, standing face to face with families facing almost impossible odds. He could have walked away. Each time, he dug in his heels, determined to help and to motivate the rest of the world to do the same.

Wayne has used his entrepreneurial spirit and the wisdom of his experiences to empower impoverished individuals to help themselves by teaching them to become micro-entrepreneurs. These folks harnessed their love for their families and their determination to have better lives, to overcome deep-seated fear and the paralysis of poverty.

Wayne is at it again. He continues to push individuals to believe they can make a difference—that their lives are part of a global tapestry of generous acts, which will create a world where compassion wins the day and fulfills families' most basic human needs.

We need more books like *Tied Together: A Pathway to Hope*. We need more people to believe that the human spirit can accomplish much more than just standing in place while our lives pass us by. I hope the stories Wayne tells in this book and the strategies he unveils here will give you the courage to help create extraordinary outcomes. We live in a world where too many people desperately need our help."

– Keith Landry, Former TV News Anchor, Orlando, FL

I understand that what Ralph LoVuolo writes below can seem like rhetorical questions, but there's a lot of power to what he asks.

I think we should all be asking, every day, what we can do to help someone else and be the change. That's a large part of what this book is about and the message that my dad wants to send to you, the reader. If you've ever had an idea, no matter how crazy or ridiculous, he wants you to believe in yourself and do it.

My dad and his team aren't the only people in the world doing social enterprise work. There are thousands of others and millions more who live a life of kindness and generosity. When each one of us who decides to help someone else, we make the world better, one life at a time.

"1. What better person to let us into his world as a humanitarian worker helping thousands?

2. What better way is there for all of us as we go about our daily work in the 'for-profit world' and at the same time develop our humanitarian side? Success in anything we undertake in life can be hard and even tough. However, with this book as our guide, we can all accomplish much.

3. How can we elevate our thoughts on how any one of us could emulate Wayne's thoughts on charity personal responsibility, and entrepreneurship?

4. How each of us can and should do our share to help our families, friends and the people we meet to improve the world in which we live. Each little bit compounds over time into positive lives for all just as Wayne has done." – **Ralph L. LoVuolo, Principal (semi-retired), The Meadows Group, Specialists in Troubled Situations**

Carrie Reichartz is another person who came to know my father through social media. You've got to think how amazing that is that people who have met him on a digital platform have become people that he considers friends or close associates.

And, what's also incredible is that my dad helped her in ways that went above and beyond what others might do when they did not know someone well. But, of course, this is the kind of person he is, but it's not something that he likes to talk about very much, so this was a story that I didn't know as close as I am to him.

In fact, a lot of these reflections and stories I did not know, including Carrie's, but it's something that I've loved to read. Each of these people has not only given my dad a gift, but they've also given a gift to his grandkids and me. All of these words and stories, help create a legacy of a life well lived in service to others.

"I was first introduced to Wayne Elsey through social media during a transition period in my life. Wayne took time, finances, and other resources and helped me during a time after I had just left my career as a lawyer and closed down my business to pursue nonprofit work in Kenya full-time and my board was turning against me in various areas. Wayne was there when I didn't think I had anywhere else to turn. His book *Almost Isn't Good Enough* was an inspiration and encouraged me as I started my work in Kenya a little more solo than I anticipated.

Wayne lives what he writes. His passion and inspiration of one person being able to change the world has changed the course of my life. After getting past the board issues, with Wayne's help and guidance, now several years later, I with my amazing team, have been able to build the first of its kind pregnancy crisis center/maternity home in an area of the world where no such place exists. Girls are being left to the streets if they are pregnant out of wedlock even if said pregnancy is the result of forced sex. Our home opened in August 2018, and we are saving babies and girls from abandonment and suicide daily.

We are soon going to launch our social entrepreneurship division of this project as our girls will each leave our center with a full year of intense counseling, a full year of vocational skills, but most importantly a full year of business training skills. This whole portion of the project has been inspired by the work Wayne has been doing all over the world and especially in Haiti.

I have learned so much from Wayne and continue to learn from him. He truly is a bridge for others who are seeking to change the world as we know it for the better. You will not want to miss this book—be inspired—and as Wayne says in every email—'YOU Matter'—YOU can and do change the world!" – **Carrie Reichartz, Founder and President, Infinitely More Life and Mercy's Light Family**

I'm fortunate to have friends that I've had in my life for years, but I also know that many people don't keep friendships that they made, especially in elementary school.

Jodi Beard's words demonstrate that we can maintain friendships that stretch all the way back to our childhoods if we only reach out. She mentions how her kids asked my dad about how their mother was in school. I'd like to let Jodi know that should I ever meet her, I want to hear her stories about my father when he was a kid. (By the way, I noticed that she didn't have a mention of my dad being a ladies' man; just saying).

"I've known Wayne since elementary school. As life would have it, time and distance separated us after high school. But, with the advent of social media at the beginning of the millennium, Wayne and I caught up with each other again.

My husband, Alan, was a Marine stationed at Camp Pendleton and we were living in Oceanside, CA; Wayne was flying through on business, and he invited us to meet him for dinner downtown in San Diego. Although we had known each other long, we were merely acquaintances by the time we graduated high school, and it had been almost twenty years since seeing each other.

Wayne had climbed the corporate ladder and had become a very successful businessman. I believe he was the CEO/President of a major footwear company, and I was a military spouse working a 9-5 job, who devoted the rest of her time playing a cheerleader to my, well, cheerleader daughter and swimmer son. Our lives' directions had taken  us on divergent paths, leaving us with little in common. Suffice to say I was a little nervous.

We met Wayne at a seafood restaurant in the San Diego harbor. And to sum the experience up, we were old acquaintances becoming new friends. We talked and laughed, cajoled about the old days. He nicknamed my daughter Lemonhead because she ate all the lemon wedges at the table and my son was given the name Aqua Boy because he was a competitive swimmer at the time, breaking pool records.

We talked about family, old friends, teachers in school, and then it happened. My kids asked what I feared. 'What was my mom like when she was a kid? Tell us about her.' I was doomed. Wayne began to tell him that he really didn't remember a whole lot, it was so long ago (he's older than me and always will be!), but he did remember one story.

One day, his brother Timmy came home from school and asked Wayne if he had been picking on me. You see, Timmy went to school with my older brother and sister and evidently, somebody (I swear to this day it wasn't me) told my brother or sister that Wayne was picking on me. Whoever it was must have told Timmy and, well, Timmy took matters into his own hands and did the big brother thing and beat Wayne up for it.

Of course, by this time my kids are giving me the business for being a tattler, and Wayne is smiling and laughing. I told Wayne then, and I continue to say to him to this day, that it wasn't me, because I would have just beat him up myself.

It's been more than fifteen years since that dinner in San Diego, and Wayne and I have continued to keep in touch and grow our friendship. Simply because we reached out to each other, into the unknown, what was once a couple of fourth graders picking and teasing at each other (and kicking each other too) has blossomed into a friendship that has been able to withstand time. We are still separated by distance, but technology has allowed us to stay close.

Twice yearly we vacation in Florida, and each time we make it a point to meet up with Wayne and Courtney if schedules permit. I have even brought other friends whom I've met while Alan was in the Marine Corps, and Wayne has welcomed them into his home and treated them as old friends (minus the kicking and teasing, of course). We are never disappointed when visiting Wayne, only when we are unable to see him.

My friendship with Wayne has taught me how important it is to reach out to one another, even if it can seem daunting. Make old acquaintances new friends, because there's a lot you might be missing in someone if you don't open your mind to the possibilities that time provides. You might just go from kicking and teasing each other in grade school, to kicking around dates and times on the calendar to meet up for lunch or dinner." – **Jodi Beard, Contracting Officer, Strategic Acquisitions Programs Directorate, DLA Aviation Richmond**

Tony Deitch has another reflection, just as an earlier one in this book, about poverty in our country and how a child has plastic bags around her feet for shoes. How can that even be possible? It's something that shouldn't be possible, neither in the U.S. nor in any country, and it's the driving force behind why my dad and his team do what they do each day.

It's incredible to me to think that there are children in our country and around the world who can't afford a pair of shoes. It's something so many of us take for granted but are so incredibly important for many reasons, including health.

"One cold January day back about 40 years ago, I had witnessed a little girl on the streets with her mother. She had plastic bags around each foot and held up with rubber bands around her ankles. No one, I thought at that moment, should ever be without footwear especially in my community.

This was the impetus for creating 'The Shoe Drive for The Homeless,' an annual drive collecting footwear in good condition and organizing an event with hundreds of volunteers that went from shelter to soup kitchen fitting the donated shoes on people in need. This happening was performed annually for several years, fitting hundreds of thousands of shoes on those in need in central Pennsylvania.

In the early 2000s, Wayne Elsey had his own personal epiphany prompting and calling him to take action. Initially creating Soles4Souls, and continuing efforts to move forward in exceptionally creative ways, all with the result of helping our fellow man, globally. Wayne's organization, with a suite of different endeavors and dedicated people who simply refuse to 'pick a side' as we are told to do in today's society and are tied into one result: Taking the 'side' of our fellow men, woman, and children in need— Helping Our Fellow Person, Worldwide!

I encourage all who want to receive the best that life

has to offer to read *Tied Together: A Pathway to Hope* and you will sense the significance and urgency to join Wayne's revolution and obtain the one of a kind sensation that helping our fellow man provides. It really is very simple and powerful!" – **Tony Deitch**

Amanda Lawrence offers us another look at my dad's work and what could be his incredible spirit.

I love this story about how he helped a woman he probably did not know auction off a simple bracelet and make it the highest bid item at a fundraiser. It's not surprising he would do that, and I'm sure it happened because he was taken by the fact that this woman was willing to do anything to raise more money, even with something as small as a bracelet.

It was for a good cause, and so my father, of course, was set on giving it his all to make something great of something so small.

"As a former executive director of a not-for-profit that partnered with Wayne Elsey's first social enterprise, Soles4Souls, I can attest to his strength of character and focused and determined passion. Wayne channels this into his newest book, *Tied Together: A Pathway to Hope*. I attempted to create a for-profit social enterprise a couple of years ago, and although the passion and plan were there, it lacked experience, knowledge, and investment, so I wish I had had his newest book in my hands before and during the creation of this company.

This book gets into the hands of talented entrepreneurs who also have a passion for making a difference in this world that it will help birth many extraordinary new for-profit social enterprises, which will, in turn, make incredible impacts on this world. I'm thankful for an author that sees that the wisdom and experience he has been given is best when shared with others so that his impact can make an even more significant ripple effect collectively with others who are impacted by his story.

One memory I have of Wayne is when he attended a fundraiser I coordinated for an international adoption agency. We had an orphanage director from Ethiopia visiting, and she was so passionate about raising money to help the orphanage, that she spontaneously got on stage and began auctioning off her bracelet. The bracelet was probably worth a couple of dollars, but Wayne joined her in her enthusiasm, and it became the highest bid of the whole night—all for that one simple bracelet offered by one very humble and gracious heart. Who knew how much that bracelet was worth to her personally. I believe Wayne was one of the only people at that event that did not look at the actual worth of that bracelet but saw the orphanage director's heart and passion for caring for the children that she tended to day in and day out, who needed our help."
– Amanda Lawrence

And now, we get the Courtney, my dad's wife. What can I say of the next reflection by Courtney?

I guess for starters, many people might not realize that my dad is married to the executive vice president of his company. The reason is simple. They keep their personal life personal, and they're about others much more than themselves.

They're union started with a meeting at a bar with Courtney giving my dad lip saying, "What are you staring at?" as she passed him. That spirit caught my dad's interest, especially because Courtney is more than a foot shorter than his 6'4" frame. She had a lot of attitude, which got my father's attention. I think he had a challenge on his radar with her!

We can say that the rest of it is history. Josh, the kids, me and especially my dad, are fortunate to call Courtney family.

"Recently I opened up the dictionary on my desk to look up the definition of the word 'character':

Definition of Character: 1. the mental and moral qualities distinctive to an individual.
And also,
2. a person in a novel, play, or movie.

Wayne's character is unlike any other I've seen in my life. He has a deeply rooted moral compass, and people who know him realize he is a 'character' who lives a life filled with vibrant color. He is fun, comical and keeps us on our toes every day! When we are with Melissa, Josh and the grands, as we like to call the kids, it is nothing but goofiness and laughter. These kids know their Doopta loves them and would fight for them as would I. I may not be blood to Melissa, Josh, Aubree, Aiden, and Jaxon, but blood is not the only quality that is necessary for a family. We are a family because of the loyalty, love, support, trust, and acceptance that exists in our relationships with each other; the accep-

tance that we are 'tied together' because we all choose this path for ourselves. It's really that simple.

We can all choose to be 'tied' to our family, friends, companies where we work and our communities. When we are bound to each other, inevitably we will find that we have ended up creating more joy and happiness in our own life because we've chosen to share our gifts.

Our journeys really do impact each other in ways that we don't always know or are visually evident. We will

TIED TOGETHER: A PATHWAY TO HOPE

never know the full extent of Wayne's impact in this world, but if there were such a thing as an 'impact meter,' I would be the first to ask that we should use it to measure the impact of Wayne's life. Maybe in YouTube views and ratings on Facebook are the way we measure impact, but somehow that doesn't seem to be sufficient.

How do you really know you're making an impact? You don't always realize it. For instance, Jackie Busch, who was Wayne's high school teacher, may not ever fully know the impact she made in Wayne's life. Without her, we may have never known the Wayne that exists today who believes in himself and the goodness and humanity of others. Just one small gesture changed the path of that young teenage boy. The words from Jackie, 'YOU Matter,' was all Wayne needed to hear. Maybe for you today it's smiling at someone you usually wouldn't, or perhaps it's volunteering your time to give a hand up to someone else.

Wayne will continue to inspire, give a hand up and show through his life that all of us, including YOU, can make a difference. It doesn't need to take money or a lot of time. Americans sit on the couch all too often in the evenings or on weekends binge-watching Netflix. Wayne does neither. In reality, we all have time. Time to spend with someone you know, someone you don't know or volunteering. Wayne has already left a legacy that our family is proud of and I suspect his grandkids will follow when they grow up.

His legacy continues through the company I have had the great pleasure to work in with Wayne. From the first day, it's been about helping the micro-entrepreneurs and the organizations that are earning funding through the shoe drive fundraisers with the Funds2Orgs Group. It's been an incredible journey watching the company grow to what we are today, through all of the many iterations we have experienced, and the people that joined us to create a fantastic culture. There are genuine love and affection between co-workers, and it's fair to say that we're one big family!

Have you ever offered to help another person or persons? I have, and I imagine most of us have helped someone else. Perhaps it's been as simple as tying someone's shoelaces, or it's creating successful social enterprises, like Wayne.

So, what's the difference between Wayne and me, or Melissa and her dad? I've helped people in offering to jump someone's car or have handed 'Cuties' to a homeless person. Melissa has offered a kind word. My hope and Melissa's has been that we hope it helps in some way, and perhaps in the short-term it does.

However, Wayne thinks differently than me or most others that I've met. What do I mean by that? Here's how. My step-dad, Chuck, and I were with Wayne several years ago, garage selling! Yes, the three of us pulled up to a house that was having a sale and there was a broken-down car in front of the house. Two ladies from Haiti were trying to get their car started again and needed a 'jump.' The owner of the house handed us the cables but also said we were not using his car for the jump. Chuck, Wayne and I sprung into action to get their van started.

After we got the car started, I thought to myself that it was awesome to help a couple of very nice ladies, and I also thought that we would continue with our day. Nope. For most of us, jumping the car would be the end of a job well done and paying kindness forward. But, I was with Wayne, and this story didn't end where most of us would finish. Wayne led an expedition to the closest auto store for a new battery to test the battery. When the test came back with the bad news that the battery was done, he quietly purchased them a new battery, with the expectation of nothing in return. Why did Wayne do this simple act of kindness? During the jump in front of the house, he got to know them and learned that the women were purchasing items to send back to Haiti to be sold on the streets by people trying to help themselves out of poverty. You see, Wayne has seen first-hand how hard the Haitian people work to take care of their families and each other. For Wayne, buying the car battery was his contribution to helping them help others he would probably never meet in Haiti, a country whose people and spirit course through his veins.

Wayne is 'tied together' to his community. Whether it's in Orlando or online, he gets a lot of requests, especially through social media to help someone out. Many national and global leaders get these types of requests.

In some cases, he can help, or he serves as the bridge to getting the proper assistance someone needs to alleviate not only the symptom of their need but also the cause of the harsh circumstances in their life. However, some requests make assumptions about who Wayne is as a person, and he doesn't honor them. For instance, one person asked for him to fly their parent's precious pet from Orlando to Chicago on his private plane. Sorry folks. Wayne doesn't have a private jet at his disposal and flies coach like most of us. Unfortunately, he couldn't help them, but my sense is that if he did have a private plane, and it was a child or person in need of an emergency medical procedure, he would do it if he could.

Wayne continually gives of himself, his time, his advice and resources. He sometimes appears to be on his phone all day every day, because he's always learning, researching or maybe someone has called to ask his advice. Simply put, Wayne makes himself available. He still goes above and beyond, even at a point in his life when he doesn't have to do it; I'm amazed because he does so many things for people, particularly when nobody is watching, and there is no fanfare.

There's a quote by John Wooden, 'The true test of a man's character is what he does when no one is watching.' Wayne doesn't do what he does to seek adoration from others; he has no ego, but what he does have is a big heart for people. He genuinely cares about people and creating circumstances that improve the lives of the one, or the many.

Hope is what he always says matters. If you give someone hope, then, they get motivated with desire and the feeling that whatever they need to happen will. In the end, that's what Wayne's most significant gift to others is... the opportunity to hope that what is desired will happen.

I hope that this book shows people that it just takes a spark, and I hope this book is also the spark you need to be 'tied together' with others wherever you are in the world." – **Courtney Eaton, Executive Vice President, Elsey Enterprises, and Wayne's Wife**

As my part of this book draws to a close, I want to express how grateful I am to have my father in my life. Unfortunately, my mom died suddenly and since her passing, not a day passes that I don't remember her. My kids

and I miss her terribly, but we're also fortunate to have the "great" Wayne Elsey in our lives. To us, he's just my dad and Doopta to my kids.

He's the guy who calls every morning to listen to what the kids have to say. He's the man who will take a plane at a moment's notice if I should ever need him. He's a leader, visionary, but he's also an ordinary person, and all of us can do what he does. Clearly, when you give of yourself and reach out with kindness to others, they remember.

There's a quote by Maya Angelou that has been noted a couple of times in this book, and there's a reason for it...it resonates and is so very true. Angelou wrote, "People may not remember exactly what you did, or what you said, but they will always remember how you made them feel."

Clearly, in everything I read and reflected in the words of so many others, is how my dad made them feel, which prompted them to write in his honor. It's a lesson I will always remember, and I hope my children will someday internalize when they one day read this book themselves, each in his or her own way and time.

POSTSCRIPT
Get Off the Couch

"I think the whole world is dying to hear someone say, 'I love you.' I think that if I can leave the legacy of love and passion in the world, then I think I've done my job in a world that's getting colder and colder by the day."
—**Lionel Richie**

Through the years, I've been fortunate to have many incredible experiences. Some have been life-changing and inspiring, such as the birth of my daughter and grandchildren. Others have been difficult to absorb. The deaths of both my father and best friend, Fran, readily come to mind. I've experienced travel, where I've had the opportunity to meet some of the celebrated leaders of our time, as well as people who have made an impact in my life because of their quiet dignity and a sense of purpose.

We live in a time of complexity, enormous innovation, and change. For some, this can be overwhelming, and perhaps that's one of the reasons we also live during a period that seems to have more than its fair share of negativity, distrust, and anger. However, I believe that humans are intrinsically good, and as we move toward a different societal paradigm that is shaking itself out, we'll come to a place that will be better. But, to get to that destination, every one of us has to step up. We have to believe. We have to act. We have to make a better world a reality, where we care for each other, even those we might never meet.

Frequently many of us don't push beyond our comfort zone because critics challenge us. Realize that critics can only criticize when you're doing something. They are looking for something to react to, and by your doing something, that alone brings out critics, but it will also bring out supporters and like-minded people. Don't be ashamed to try and fail, and even to be criticized for it. It doesn't matter—ever. Every moment you're trying, doing, and yes, also failing, is a learning opportunity. Just learn, improve and keep moving forward.

In closing, I want to go back to Dan Pallotta's words about being ridiculous. He's right. Each one of us can be ridiculous and create organizations, including businesses and social enterprises, that reach incredible heights of potential. Every one of us can be absurd in having the idea that has never been done or been well done until we've done it. I love what Dan said, "The most sophisticated things I've ever seen in my life—the most intelligent solutions to the greatest technical challenges in history—all came from someone being ridiculous. Ridiculous is what really tests us. Stretches us. Forces us to use the full measures of our intelligence, creativity, fortitude, and strength."

Candidly, I couldn't have said it better myself. When we don't dream the big dreams and execute consistently with a group of other believers, so much of what could have been lies in the trash heap of what could have been. That's not who we should be. So, even if you're in a place where you haven't done what you've wanted to do to make the degree impact you want to make, don't waste time looking through the rearview mirror and center your vision through the windshield. There's a reason why it's the biggest window in a car that is propelling itself forward. All you have to do is get off the couch and move forward without fear about the unknown and what lies ahead. The journey is the "why" it's all worth it, along with the people you meet along the way. The destination, truly, doesn't matter.

If you have a burning fire within you to do something that extends beyond yourself to people in your community and even the world, I say do it. All you need is an idea, precise execution that is focused and consistent, and a team of people with you who can see what you see, even if it's only one other person.

I've done it.

Dan's done it.

My grandkids will do it.

You can do it too.

AUTHOR'S NOTES

"Please think about your legacy because you are writing it every day."
– **Gary Vaynerchuk**

The following endorsements and words that are part of this final section are greatly appreciated. Candidly, reading all of these words and the others that were placed earlier in the book was a bit overwhelming. Again, I'm personally very grateful, as is my family, including Melissa, Courtney, Josh and my grandchildren for the kindness and generosity demonstrated to me by so many people. YOU Matter. Thank you.

– **Wayne Elsey**

"I am glad to endorse any project of Wayne's and definitely this one. Our families are longtime friends. We reconnected years ago, and he has inspired me so. In his giving nature but even more as the friend he's been. Someone you can always count on in life." – **Eddie Crosslin**

"I had the immense pleasure of working with Wayne and his team at Soles4Souls several years ago and truly loved his passion, zeal, and energy. What stood out to me about Wayne was that he never sees a challenge, only an opportunity and reading these passages helped me reflect on the things that truly inspire me to be step up and do what I can to change the world." – **Shane E. Burkett**

"Wayne's book will inspire you to establish personal, face to face contact with the people that matter in your life. It's all too easy to send a quick Happy Birthday tweet to a friend or relative. But in this time of turmoil and discord, Wayne encourages us to make the world a better place by starting to make connections with our inner circle. From there, we can all reach out and write letters to our elected officials, mow an elderly neighbor's yard or start a grass-roots volunteer organization. Since we're all 'tied together,' let's be 'tied together' to improve the world according to our strengths and talents." – **Silvana Clark, Speaker/Author/Brand Ambassador**

"This book couldn't be timed any better. We are being torn apart by politics, affiliations, religions, orientations—but there are things that bind us together. This book reminds you that we are ALL human and the traits that truly tie us together. A must read with actionable steps to keep those in your life tied not divided." – **Brian Williams, President & Founder, Think Kindness**

"I'm so excited about this latest book from Wayne. I'm very proud that someone as inspiring and motivating as Wayne calls me his friend. He has set the gold standard by living a philanthropic life and taking action on humanitarian needs. If you're looking for that inspiration in yourself, you'll find it in the passages of his books. He reminds us that we're all human and that we all matter. And he means that!" – **Jodi Beard, Contracting Officer, Strategic Acquisitions Programs Directorate, DLA Aviation Richmond**

"Wayne is a social entrepreneur and visionary that has built success by thinking differently, pushing the norms of his industry, and teaching people how to provide hope in places that many leave unnoticed.

Part of the journey over the years, I am inspired by Wayne's latest endeavor, *Tied Together: A Pathway to Hope*. As the consummate visionary, Wayne is addressing a topic that is critically relevant and providing a bridge of hope. *Tied Together: A Pathway to Hope* is a must read as we live in a divided world that needs to learn how to work together, listen, share, and build community through respectful and thoughtful interaction. This book provides the foundation to better days ahead and the discussion that needs to begin now." – **Joseph Dulaney, Educational Technology Sales Executive**

"Wayne and I were both entrenched in separate corners with relief efforts post-Katrina. Not knowing each other but, by his words, 'Doing better and being better,' as volunteers in the tragedies that struck so many. How fortunate that we were placed together years later in 2011, during my presidency of the Million Dollar Round Table Foundation. Sole4Souls was the designated charity that year and appeared on our main stage to enlighten our worldwide members of how something as simple as a pair of shoes makes an impact around the world.

Wayne is a true example of how someone with a heart of passion for hurting souls can make such a significant difference. I've called on him several times when volunteering for other disaster relief efforts and he was quick to respond and helped by connecting me to numerous charities who came to our aid. He's a leader. A social entrepreneur. A man with tremendous social impact. He delivers hope with great respect and acceptance of all.

I would encourage you to read about his outreach and his work. We are truly all 'tied together' and this book describes succinctly how to bridge those gaps with humankind. Congratulations and best wishes to a dear friend, Wayne Elsey." – **Robelynn H. Abadie, CEO, Abadie Financial Services, LLC, Past International President, MDRT Foundation**

"I have known Wayne for 30 years. He has always been a person who has a positive approach to life and wants to make a difference in the lives of others. His passion for life drives him to lead others to do really big things that will truly improve the living conditions for others.

Since that fateful day in 2004 when Wayne saw that shoe wash up on shore in the newscast of the devastating tsunami in Indonesia, Wayne was never the same man. He jumped into action because he knew that as humans 'We Can Do Anything We Want to Do.' He did it and has helped countless people in developing countries. My hope for you who read this book is to become inspired by Wayne's words and make your own story. Step out of your comfort zone. Live a life of passion and purpose and leave your special mark in this world." – **Brian Leary, Dollar General Corporation, Long Time Friend and former colleague of Wayne**

"Highly energetic and indefatigable! An entrepreneurial force of nature! If you've met Wayne Elsey or been around him, you know what I mean. As an experienced wine and food marketer and public relations executive, I've known Wayne for 7+ years. We've worked together on several initiatives including a highly innovative partnership that gave 600,000 pairs of shoes to people in need, along with the unprecedented launch of a successful wine brand. We traveled together to both west and east coasts, meeting with top national media, government officials, business owners, community leaders, and millennials. Above all, I was impressed with Wayne's ability to engage one-on-one with diverse folks, command a room and get people on board with ideas—even people who were initially on different pages.

His latest book *Tied Together: A Pathway to Hope* is a roadmap for those of us who want to leave the planet healthier than we found it, who believe in the power of communications and engagement and who want to know more about for-profit social enterprises that work. Elsey cuts through the drama and self-righteousness that are hallmarks of today's divided world inviting a focus on humanity's common needs and aspirations. Through hard-earned lessons and experience, Wayne demonstrates that we can do better and be better as individuals and society.

Need a dose of inspiration? This book is a must read, and I highly recommend it to all my colleagues." – **Patricia Schneider, President, Patricia Schneider Consulting**

"Again, Wayne has produced an invaluable source for his readers. I feel blessed that I am able to work side by side with Wayne and learn from him daily, but to be able to get inside his head and learn from his writings is an asset for us all. I will share with many of my personal and professional friends." – **Yvonne Keller, Chief Operating Officer, Elsey Enterprises**

"Every once in a while, someone comes along who has the uncanny ability not only to recognize the ties that we all share as human beings but also helps us imagine the great things that we can accomplish with a collective mind. In his book, *Tied Together: A Pathway to Hope*, Wayne Elsey urges us to reach deep within our souls, put aside our differences, and grasp for the one thing that truly matters in life—the human connection." – **Sophia P. Ryder, M. Ed., Gifted Resource Teacher, Stafford County Public Schools**

"Watching the devastation unfold as the 2004 tsunami in Indonesia wreaked havoc, Wayne Elsey left a successful career and made a full-time commitment to finding means to fund humanitarian service. Driven by a desire to involve people in this passion, he is masterful at motivating and mobilizing funding for the poor. His writing communicates his heart and is a significant contribution to this effort. Read this book and be inspired by his story." – **David Lorency**

"I met Wayne in 2008 when we partnered on a project with Soles4Souls at the church where I was on staff. I was blown away by Wayne's optimism and desire to change the world. We're all told that we can change the world, but we get bogged and blinded by life, bills, work, deadlines, and the constant continuation of days that feel less like changing the world and more like surviving the day.

We may work in a for-profit or a not for profit, the deluge of life is the same, and the results are the same, we stop living like we can do more, we stop believing that what we are doing matters, and we stop looking ahead in hope. Bill Gates said, 'Most people overestimate what they can do in one year and underestimate what they can do in ten years.' You can change the world. It's work, but it can happen. In this book, Wayne outlines some quality lessons from the fight and shares how God has used him to change the world. Glean from his wins and losses. Most importantly, get hope to lift your eyes up, believe in your calling, and do the work because the world is waiting." – **Trey Brunson, Communications Director, Southeast Christian Church, Executive Producer, Run the Race**

"Another excellent read from Wayne Elsey about the tremendous positive impact of giving back. He shows his audience why giving is important and tells them how to use their talents and resources best to do good in the world.

When I traveled with Wayne to Haiti following the 2010 earthquake, I witnessed his compassionate nature firsthand in every interaction he had with people in need. He has a unique gift to make people feel dignity in receiving." – **Rita Polidori O'Brien**

"There is nothing small about Wayne Elsey. Not the way he appears, standing at well over 6 feet tall. Not the way he thinks, developing strategies designed to help those in need. And not the way he acts, continuing to create and execute programs that deliver results. Everything this man does looms large in a soft and personal way. Wayne has an enormous heart, and he cares deeply. You answer when he calls. You listen when he speaks. And you give when he asks. Wayne has big ideas.

Tied Together: A Pathway to Hope is today's big idea. A must-read for anyone interested in doing their part in making a social impact. In this book, we are reminded that strength is in numbers and numbers add up. Kindness and generosity come in a gazillion different ways and they all matter. One by one, our deliberate acts can make a difference in the lives of people in need. Each of us, if so inspired, can impact the future of those less fortunate purposefully and positively. Some contributions are more significant than others, and they all matter. We are all human beings. So very much the same more than we are different. Collectively, we have the power to make the world a better place, 'tied together' in more ways than one." – **Dana Rosenberg, Consultant, Marketing Communications + Strategic Partnerships**

"Wayne Elsey has been an entrepreneur that found a way to offer hope to the world in a physical way as well as a spiritual, and emotional way. When starting the business Soles4Souls, Wayne put into action what it takes to be a business developer as well as finding a way to meet a universal cause and at the same time enrich the heart and give hope to the hopeless and faith to the fearful. As Wayne went on to start another business he, once again, found a need both physically, emotionally, and in a business format to help others do what he had done with their heartfelt calling. His entrepreneurial leadership and writing style are definitely 'teach a man to fish, and he too can be a fisherman.'" – **Paula Foster**

"Wayne Elsey has been such an inspiration on his journey to help others in every facet of life. Not only has he diligently strived to stop the spread of disease through the donation of shoes to those in need. He has also been a leader and a true example of how everyone can help! From starting your organization to supporting your location organizations, this book will benefit the entrepreneur and advocate alike to take a step forward in helping those around you!" – **Priscilla Willis, Director, Oak Hall**

"I met Wayne many years ago when we served on the Board of Directors together of a fledgling company in Nashville, TN. During that time, and after that we have touched base with one another on many occasions. Through the years, Wayne was always up to some new endeavor for which he had great enthusiasm. He possesses fast-stream of multifaceted thoughts, which allow him to talk with great speed and excitement. I have often said Wayne can speak faster than I can hear!

However, if one can keep up with his flow of ideas, one feels like they are on a swiftly moving river, which is bumpy and scary at first, but if you hang on, you'll be carried to realms that surprise, and expand, and often reveal views and vistas that are new to one's imagination and perceptions. He is a master of creativity.

Wayne now brings forth yet another stream of ideas and perceptions that will transform his readers' mindset hopefully for the good of humankind. I wish his readers the best in this new adventure." – **Ronda C Weinstock, Ph.D.**

"For the 12+ years that we've known Wayne, he has always inspired us with his entrepreneurial savvy, and even more so by his desire and intent to serve others in need. In this book, he shares valuable and meaningful information that we look forward to applying to our business venture as well as our growing nonprofit. Few people get to experience the level of success that Wayne has achieved; this book offers a unique opportunity to learn from a great visionary who believes in making the world a better place." – **Cristina Nardozzi Buehrer, Miss Massachusetts USA 2005, Co-Founder, Model Makers Group, Program Director - A Model Patient 501(c)(3) and Tara Darby Rasheta, Miss AL USA 2004, Co-Founder, Model Makers Group Founder - A Model Patient 501(c)(3)**

"We want to highly recommend that you get Wayne Elsey's new book, *Tied Together: A Pathway to Hope*. We've known Wayne for many years and have watched with admiration how he has created multiple organizations that all had one thing in common: to make a difference in people lives that would then make a difference in the world. As an activist and entrepreneur, Wayne has been a strategic thinker and then activator that from whom many people have learned. In this book, you'll discover further ways of how you can create a more impactful enterprise, for the betterment of your life and the world. Get this book. Read this book. Apply this book. Then watch your own difference making quotient and experience rise dramatically." – **Pastor David & Caron Loveless, First Baptist Church Orlando**

"Wayne Elsey Capitalist with a moral conscience. A man that does business for profit. So that he can use his benevolent nature, to enhance other's lives. Wayne lives by a concept I define as 'Value for Value.' His businesses generate profit (value), to which he adds benevolent value to the world." – **Dominic Colone III**

"Wayne Elsey has written a must-read guide for anyone considering social entrepreneurship...Read this book, and you will learn from one of the most innovative and successful names in the business.

I have many fond memories of Wayne, too many to narrow down just one favorite. As a close family friend, I have had the privilege of enjoying his company on numerous occasions over the years. Perhaps the thing that I admire most about him is his dedication to his family. The family is so important, and in the age of social media, it can often be neglected. Wayne provides a prime example to follow of how one should care for their loved ones and support them. It is a great honor to know him and always a pleasure to spend time with him and his beautiful family." – **Caroline B. Raymond, BA, COC, CPC**

"Wayne has been an inspiration to small business and entrepreneurs such as myself. His work with Funds2Orgs is a true testament of hard work and passion leading to success. His dedication to our work in *Fostering Families Today* only furthers his dedication to important partnerships. Wayne's thoughts, partnership, and friendship are truly an inspiration to us all. Thank you, Wayne, for all you do!" – **Bryan Curiel, Business Development Manager, Fostering Media Connections**

"This book is a call to action to humble ourselves and to work together in a united effort with others to create hope and sustainable change. The next generation is looking for people who will listen. Will you be that listening ear?" – **Kylie Rickards, Founder & Owner at Kylie Creative, Special Projects at 521 Creative**

"Melissa and I were college roommates at Mary Baldwin College. Wayne was the CEO of Soles4Souls, and Melissa was currently leading a Soles-4Souls organization at the college. I've known Wayne for almost 10 years, and he has truly been inspiring to my family and me. I am impressed with his ability to help others and am touched by his life and admiration for Melissa, his grandchildren, and his son in law. He has helped my husband and me by offering kind and motivational words that helped us to continue to move forward. The friendship I have with Melissa is one I will cherish forever. Melissa's personality is like Wayne's—giving, selfless and positive." – **Roxanne Bradley Lovelace**

"I have been fortunate enough to know Wayne for over 20 years. And I am humbled to be able to call out his contributions and his altruistic acts. Wayne is, and seems to have always been, called to do great things; his vision, his call to action, and his tireless good-works make him a pioneer in the footwear industry. Wayne has taken the mission of making sure that everyone has shoes on their feet and has made a huge difference. What greater legacy could one man have? Wayne is smart, kind, caring, and a true philanthropist." – **Beth Gordon, Director of Sales**

"Wayne realized early on the most effective way to increase love in the world is not to separate ourselves from the suffering, but to let the needs of others evoke love in us. The needs we witness will pull us toward love, toward generosity and compassion. We may prefer to remain aloof and detached, but that's not the way. The way, as Wayne has discovered, is to risk the attachments of loving, serving and giving which secretly deposit much-needed faith and happiness into our soul. This experience then quickly morphs into love for others, and the circle soon widens making clear we are all 'tied together.'" – **Rev. Cherie Larkin, Spiritual Growth Studio**

"I just wanted to share a few words and thoughts that I have in regards to Wayne Elsey. I have known Wayne for nearly a year, and in this short time, I have found a person who is truly a visionary. Wayne really sees the big picture and knows how to seek out individuals who may not have always had the best opportunities. Wayne can quickly see potential in individuals like a diamond in the rough. With Wayne's enterprise Funds2Orgs he offers a truly unique opportunity for individuals, small and large groups to 'go outside of the box' and make a difference not just in their lives but also in the lives of strangers halfway around the world. He has been able to supply not only goods to individuals in need but also truly changed lives! In life, sometimes, it is easy to 'stay in your lane' it's not as easy to change lanes and make an impact, and that is what Wayne Elsey does every day." – **Kevin Albert, Fundraising Coach, Funds2Orgs Group**

"Now and then a book comes along to remind us that life is short. There are tremendous needs in our community and world, and we don't have to look very far to see this first hand. Wayne Elsey was able to see this at a young age and figured out how he could make an impact—to serve humankind with his unique abilities and network. Whether it's for-profit or nonprofit, we all have the ability to provide hope, to leave our mark before moving on—if you need a little motivation to get started, read *Tied Together: A Pathway to Hope.*" – **John Licata, Vice President, Vida Shoes International**

"After working with Wayne and Funds2Orgs over the years, my American Soldier Network has lived the 'tied together' philosophy. Our veteran/military organization collects shoes that end up in developing countries; however, our efforts that benefit those overseas raises money for our efforts here in the USA for our military and veterans. Our military who do so much for the impoverished overseas, yet you never hear about that here at home, ultimately continuing to give back to those less fortunate through our shoe drive efforts. Just goes to show how we truly are all 'tied together." - **Annie Nelson, Advocate, TV Host, Keynote Speaker & Founder American Soldier Network**

"Wayne is innovative, creative, smart and meticulous. Always bringing the best out of people and reminding them that they matter, and they are appreciated. Above all, Wayne is a philanthropist, and a giver who cares about people here at home and abroad by supporting and encouraging missions for the best of humanity." – **Moe Hachem, CEO, Coastal Export International**

"Wayne is an exceptionally gifted leader. Having the opportunity to work with him for several years, I personally saw what an intentional caring leader he is. His insight on how to build an organization and treat people is beyond the norm for any company. We have adopted several of his practices in our company today. A great story to share would be the time Wayne and I were in Colorado Springs, and Wayne got the people in the room where we were to take off their shoes and donate them at the altar. Then they went home barefoot. It was a truly impactful evening.
     Wayne is an exceptionally gifted leader. Having the opportunity to work with him for several years, I personally saw what an intentional caring leader he is. His insight on how to build an organization and treat people is beyond the norm for any company. We have adopted several of his practices in our company today." – **Sean Michael Lewis CEO/Founder of Tier Level**

"I love people who live with purpose and passion. That describes Wayne as much as anyone I know. This book will help ignite in you a passion for living beyond yourself in creative ways you probably never imagined. And thus, experience fun, joy, empathy, meaning, and deep satisfaction beyond your wildest dreams." – **Mike Breaux Teaching Pastor Real Life Church, Eastside Church, Christ Church of the Valley SoCal**

"I first met Wayne Elsey approximately eleven years ago when he was serving on a board for one of my corporate clients. I was taken by his clever sense of humor and was highly impressed with his resourcefulness, creativity, and his people and leadership skills. As I got to know him better, I was even more impressed with his heart for charity and his compassion for others. Wayne is a highly successful philanthropic entrepreneur who, among other things, founded and built Soles4Souls, a highly successful charity. Wayne is a visionary for philanthropic causes and has a rare talent for motivating others to pay it forward. Wayne has a heart for helping others, and he is always seeking ways to make the world a better place." – **Nader Baydoun, Baydoun & Knight, PLLC**

"Watching Wayne since we were in grade school, he has been living what I feel should be the American dream, serving and investing in others, bringing hope so they can be the best they can be. He believes in putting extra into the ordinary and freely shares from a deep well of experience. Would you join him and be 'tied together' so you also can be a pathway to hope. I sincerely and highly endorse Wayne's new book." – **Tammy Cleveland, a sister in Christ and fellow classmate**

"Wayne Elsey is one of those rare individuals who can act with his heart and his head simultaneously. He has the emotional intelligence to analyze what's going on and come up with solutions that are pragmatic, heartfelt and perfectly appropriate. When he founded Soles4Souls in 2004, he saw people in Sri Lanka who were suffering. And he also understood that people in America wanted to help and created a way for them to do so in a quick, meaningful manner. Wayne has taken the notion of caring for others, and that translated that into a creative real-life solution for today's world. His book in an inspirational road map to social entrepreneurship." – **Mark Sullivan, Former Group Editor & Publisher Footwear News, Co-Founder of The Running Event Trade Show**

"Several years ago, our organization Kids to Love hosted a shoe drive. Our goal was to collect 6,000+ pairs of shoes, a pair to represent each child in foster care in the state of Alabama. Once collected, we took the shoes to our state capital and lined the steps. When Wayne and his team heard about our drive, they offered to trade the used shoes for new shoes. A new pair of shoes for every foster child in the state of Alabama! What an amazing gift for our kids! Since then Wayne and I have stayed connected on social media, and he has been a supporter of our work serving children in foster care. Wayne has a gift to capture the heart for service while using business strategies for success." – **Lee Marshall, CEO/Founder, Kids to Love Foundation**

"Do you need ideas for your organization's fundraising? Read this book! Do you want to know how you can help someone secure a livelihood in a developing market? Read this book! I've been following Wayne Elsey's service and commitment to improving the lives of others for over a decade.

Read this book and let him inspire you to take action now." – **Kent Moss, GIK Director, Feed the Children**

"I've have had the pleasure of knowing Wayne for 20 + years. I've been privileged to watch him succeed through the corporate world and ultimately where his passion lies, through entrepreneurship and philanthropy. Wayne's drive and leadership with his nonprofit work have had a positive impact on countless persons. I'm looking forward to reading his new book and am excited to learn about his latest advice on making the world a better place for us all." – **Brian McKee, Software Consultant**

"I have watched Wayne Elsey perform with non-stop creativity for over 30 years. He not only thinks well beyond the conventional, but he has also had the courage to act on his ideas, yielding enormous benefits for the underprivileged, tragedy-stricken, and many others in need of a boost to their business and nonprofits." – **David DiPasquale, director, both for-profit and nonprofit organizations, consultant, CEO counselor**

"Beyond food and shelter, everyone needs footwear. Wayne's selfless and creative approach in creating a sharing vehicle for footwear creates a sense of community in sharing for others." – **Matthew Rubel, Chairman Mid-Ocean Partners Private Equity Consumer Group**

"I have gained valuable life lessons by learning from Wayne's unique perspective on business. His positive outlook and forward-thinking approach are some of his greatest strengths. Definitely read his book, as you'll be a better person for having done so." – **Kyle Redmond Berner, Founder and Chief Traveler, Feelgoodz**

"Each person comes into this world, packed with unlimited capacity. He or She can accomplish wonders and miracles. There is nothing in life more exhilarating than to achieve something important and to achieve it with excellence. Wayne Elsey is a pioneer, years ahead of his time in creating human achievement. Wayne that not only provides relief for those in need around the globe but also develops sustainable business models for generations yet unborn." – **Greg A. Tunney, Chairman Two Ten Footwear Foundation, Chairman FDRA-Footwear Distributors and Retailers of America, Global President Wolverine Worldwide Corporation-NYSX, President and CEO RG Barry Corporation-NASDAQ**

"With *Tied Together: A Pathway to Hope*, Wayne Elsey has penned a must-read for any do-gooder. Here comes a book that will expand your capacities and make you reconsider what you think you know about hope." – **Derin Cag, Founder of Richtopia.com & Co-Founder of MarketingRunners.com**

"Wayne and I have been lifelong friends; his family was our neighbors, and his mother babysat my sister and me. They did however move, and some years later we also moved to the same area. He and his brother, Timmy, were the only people we knew our age, so we reconnected and often played tennis, went to movies and out for pizza. Wayne helped my sister get her first job. As Wayne grew in his life and career, he still would call and stop by to visit when in town. If he flew in, he always stopped to speak to my dad at the airport. He has always been a caring and giving person, and it was no surprise he has made it his life's work. A truly inspiring and fun person to be around. I'm really proud to consider him more family than friend." – **Debbie Dement**

"I'm looking forward to reading *Tied Together: A Pathway to Hope*. The preface kept my attention, and I wanted to read more. Wayne is very admirable. He started at the bottom and worked his way up the ladder, all the while having a family in which he loves and is proud of in his life. This book will be an inspiration to many." – **Linda Crist**

"I've really enjoyed working with Wayne—He's a terrific entrepreneur and a great client. I asked Wayne for advice for breaking into the K-12 market, and he went above and beyond with providing me resources to support that project." – **Rafi Norburg, President, Nexus Marketing**

"I am grateful for Wayne's relentless commitment to a life of compassion and community and humble learning and joyful activism. If any of those qualities evoke desire in your spirit—read on!" – **John C. Ortberg, Pastor, Menlo Church**

"If you are interested in starting a for-profit business that is grounded in making an impact in the world, then Wayne Elsey's new book, *Tied Together: A Pathway to Hope* is a must read." – **Diana Marsh, Digital Marketing Strategist**

"*Tied Together: A Pathway to Hope* was a great reminder for me that no matter what the issues of the day are in any city around the world, on any given day, we all have more in common than differences.

With that common ground, there are so many ways to pay it forward, and they have a lot less to do with how much money you have, and so much more to do with consistently in seeking to lead and inspire others to make a positive impact in what they are truly passionate. Thanks for the re-inspiration that I needed!" – **Keith Winsell, President, World Mint Gold**

"I first met Wayne in the early '90s. He was the Sales Manager for Lake of the Woods footwear. We called it 'Lake of the Who.' Wayne was a witty, worldly, and sincere person. It was quickly evident that he was overqualified for the role and bigger things were in his future. It wasn't too long until he was President of Nautilus Footwear and then Kodiak Footwear. It was exciting to see Wayne start Soles4Souls and move into philanthropy work. I'm sure the best is yet to come for Wayne and society will be better for it due to his dedication and selfless humane work. I'm glad to call Wayne a friend." – **David Dietel, Merchandise Buyer, The TJX Companies**

"Wayne will be accurately remembered by many as a mentor, social entrepreneur, accomplished marketer, etc. but the best gift and memory he ever gave me was his friendship. Life threw me several, personal and professional, curveballs over the past seven years and Wayne was always my go-to person for advice and ultimately the calm to my storm. 'A friend loves at all times' is one of my favorite biblical passages and one that reminds me of my friend, Wayne Elsey." – **Goose Lopez-Torres, President & Founder, Complete the Pair, LLC**

"Forty plus years ago, I was riding a school bus with Wayne and had no idea what a powerhouse he would become. His latest book will truly speak to that part of your soul that shelters your humanity and compassion. It will serve to inspire you to be not one grain of sand on the beach that is easily swept away but to be one of the millions of grains of sand that can be a berm to protect yourselves and those you love from the raging storms. I agree with him when he speaks to our generation being a catalyst to catapult our children and their children into a future where kindness, benevolence, and respect overpower the senseless rage of greed and selfishness that has crept into our society. Let us all find our moral compass as Wayne has and find our true North as a whole and make this journey together." – **Dianne Strother, Former Classmate**

"If you're like me, you look at the many needs in the world and wish there was something you could do about it. But often the needs are so over-whelming that we give up, turn away and go back to our lives.

Wayne Elsey inspires us to see that indeed it is possible that each of us can make a difference, no matter where we live or what we have. It's a vision that makes things happen—seeing possibilities before us. Thank you, Wayne, for showing us that in small or large ways, we can change the world." **– Nancie Carmichael, Author of "The Unexpected Power of Home" and many other books and Publisher, Deep River Books**

"Knowing Wayne from back in our Stride Rite days makes me more than proud to see how Wayne has become, not only a friend but definitely a mentor to me and so many. Looking forward to Wayne's new book and know how many will continue to prosper from his love of humanity for the world. His strengths are so comforting and rewarding and will always be grateful for his friendship, generosity, and kindness to near and far. Just another nice thing Wayne's caring heart did a couple of months ago, Wayne had sent me a beautiful edible arrangement for the loss of my best friend. Who would ever do this? Wayne did. He is a great and caring person. I could go on. I just wanted to say that he is a man who holds no boundaries for the kindness of humankind." **– Janice "Jan" Ramos, Former Co-Worker and Forever Friend, Quincy, MA**

"As I read the excerpt from Wayne Elsey's new book *Tied Together: A Pathway to Hope,* three things come to mind. Several years ago, in the Art Museum in Australia, I bought a tea towel saying: 'I could do that. Yeah, but you didn't.' Wayne Elsey is one of those people who did and does do it. On the one hand, Wayne Elsey is an ordinary human being just like any of us—husband, father, and grandfather. On the other hand, Wayne Elsey does extraordinary things and, as such, inspires us, ordinary folks, to do inspiring things. He gives us hope. I have known Wayne Elsey since he started Soles4Souls. What I remember is the credit card I used that some-how, like Wayne, was both ordinary and extraordinary. I could use it like any other ordinary Visa or Mastercard, and on the other hand, every time I used it, it did something extraordinary—it supported Soles4Souls!"
– Bernice Todres, M.A., LFABI, Mindfulness Teacher

"From the first time I met my friend, Wayne Elsey, I knew he was a man with a heart full of hope. Hope for those less fortunate, hope for his family, hope for our country and hope for our world. In *Tied Together: A Pathway to Hope,* his insight encourages all of us to have hope, face the risks it takes to overcome challenges and make a difference." **– Jenny Hinton, Recycling Professional, and Long Time Friend**

"If you've ever thought about making a significant social impact, then this book is for you. Wayne is a visionary. He created Soles4Souls, a nonprofit social enterprise that creates sustainable jobs and provides relief through the distribution of shoes and clothing around the world. In this book, Wayne shares how individuals can make a difference in the world and provides the roadmap to accomplish this. This book is useful for anyone with a desire to impact the people around them." **– Andrew Doan, M.D., Ph.D.**

"Wayne Elsey is one of the very few people I know with the potential and the resources to enhance the world. There are no excuses, no misconceptions, only dedication, determination, and a relentless drive to improve the lives of others." **–Heather Hackett, HeatherHackett.com**

"I've known and worked with Wayne for many years, and his creativity, insights, and wisdom never cease to amaze me. But even more, I'm in awe of his positivity. He sees the best in every situation…and in every person. When I think of Wayne, I'm reminded of the story of the little boy who was such a hopeless dreamer that his parents wanted to teach him a life lesson for his birthday. Instead of buying a present, they filled his room with 2 feet of horse manure. They then told him he had a birthday present waiting in his bedroom. His parents watched as he opened the door and just stood there, studying the manure. After some time, he turned around and with an enormous smile, said, 'A pony! Where there's manure, this must be a horse!' In *Tied Together: A Pathway to Hope*, Wayne Elsey will help YOU find the ponies in your life!" **– Jeff Tikson, Founder, TiksonDirect**

"It wasn't until I stopped pretending to know everything that I finally was able to learn anything. I'm not ashamed of that. I don't regret anything about it. That was my personal growth process. That was how I stumbled upon the man I am today.

I've learned much from working and walking alongside Wayne Elsey over the years. I've learned compassion. I've developed deeper gratitude for the things I have. Most importantly, I uncovered the power I have to help others. It is a power you also possess.

You see, happiness isn't about how much you can cram into your own little corner of the world. Happiness is about reaching corners far from your own and bringing happiness and comfort to those who call those corners home. I'll never know everything. But I know enough to do my part for change. And I know that power is within all of us. Wayne ignited my desire to invoke change in this world, and he will do the same for you.

Read his book. Absorb his message. Share it with your children. Change IS possible." – **Todd Newton, Daytime Emmy Award-winning TV personality and author of "Life In The Bonus Round"**

"*Tied Together: A Pathway to Hope* immerses you in your own humanness, calls your spirit to action. Wayne Elsey, a writer, philanthropist, humanitarian gives you the reader not only inspiration but also the tools for magnificent change. Not just read but a challenge to step away from the so many things that divide us, and not just coexist, but become cohesive as humans and create a better—no a heart-filled reality. Move from desire to action, feel your human spirit awaken and create the dream."
– SkyHawk Fadigan, MD

"I began working with Wayne in 2013 as he was trying to navigate the complex workings of the Illinois regulations pertaining to charities. I was two years into my own entrepreneurial venture as a solo practicing attorney in Illinois. Wayne was just starting to expand and grow his venture Funds2Orgs. It was a perfect match. We grew together and supported each other. Without his guidance and support, I would not be where I am today.

I have been continually astounded by Wayne's optimism, constant expansion and desire to change the world, essentially one shoe at a time. You too can change the world. Read this book. In it, Wayne outlines how to make a lasting impact on the world around you and to help others. Everyone can make a difference, but you must choose the path that is important to you and makes a lasting impact." **– Jessica M. Wojtowicz Heston, Esq.**

"I've spent the last 30 years of my life helping nonprofits raise millions of dollars for their missions. Through the years, I've met a handful of people who I consider true innovators who understand the nonprofit space and have impacted both the charity and the people they serve. Wayne comes with a savvy business approach built on maximizing benefits for those he works with and support. He has a multifaceted approach to strategic planning, marketing, and fundraising which enable him to create a unique company unmatched by his peers and a greater vision toward the changes coming to the sector in the future. I find that his energy and collaborative spirit will continue to serve him and his company well. If you want to get an insight into the future of fundraising and where others will follow this is a must read." – **Paul D'Alessandro, President and CEO, D'Alessandro, Inc.**

"I have known and worked with Wayne both as a board member and as a trusted friend—though it's tough to tell the two apart. In either instance, you get straightforward honesty and compassion all wrapped into one. He sees the world through the lens of his inner soul and connects to others on a level of honesty and integrity that is truly rare.

Great masterminds like Napoleon Hill with *Think And Grow Rich* and Norman Vincent Peale with *The Power of Positive Thinking* have written about the most effective ways to succeed in life. It is rare to meet someone in today's world that actually lives by those tenets. Wayne Elsey built a modern-day success story with his business around 'The Law of Reciprocity,' benefitting the masses and enabling lasting change in many of the lives of the people he touched. He lives this law in his own personal life, and it only takes a conversation to realize his insights and attain guidance for your situation. Reading his book will enable you to personally experience these same thoughts and perspectives from his life experiences that I am certain will have you saying, 'Wow.'" – **Kenny Markanich, President, Capital Apparel**

"I first met Wayne 30 years ago when he hired me to work for him at Stride Rite. He took a chance on me then, to bring me on as an Assistant Manager and worked with me to grow and to learn how to motivate people. With his help and encouragement, I moved up to manager, moved within the company several times and had a great career with them. We stayed in contact even after he left Stride Rite to move on to bigger and better things and I was excited when he reached out to me to work with him at Funds2Orgs. I always saw myself as a middle-manager, one who got things done, but not much of a leader. I tend to coddle people too much! Wayne saw me differently and has helped me grow as a leader with our team, helping me to see more potential in myself and to grow as a person. Wayne is always quick to point out the best in everyone he meets and works with them to get to their highest potential. I am truly blessed to be able to be a member of his team as well as able to call him my friend!" – **Donna Paulus, Vice-President of Client Relations, Funds2Orgs Group**

"From one 'shoe dog' to another…Wayne and I go way back in the shoe industry, with him being our salesman representing some of the vendors of the footwear that our small independent Midwest shoe stores carried.

A friendship ensued, and while I remained focused on our shoe stores, I watched as Wayne's perspective in the shoe industry changed, from representing and selling footwear to retailers, to representing footwear as a means of charity, goodwill, sustenance, protection and a way of life for those that had/have fallen on extreme circumstances. Footwear was at the 'sole' of Wayne for as long as I have known him. My family and I wish him well on this new journey." – **Todd and Lori Vanderloop, Vanderloop's Shoes, Inc.**

"We met Wayne Elsey many years ago when he was contemplating ending his career with a shoe company. Although it appeared to us as a financial risk, he had a vision of helping others, using his knowledge and experience in the shoe business.

We watched and accompanied him in several of his events to distribute shoes etc. We were overwhelmed by the response of the poor and homeless at these events. He always saw the need and continued to pursue his mission.

The results of his wonderful imagination and dedication to hard work are evident in what we all see today.

We have many stories to tell, some funny and some very emotional. Wayne is a TRUE friend! He never forgets you and his kindness and thoughtfulness have been something we will always cherish.

We wish him all that life can give him. Love you, Wayne." – **Don and Carol Hamelin**

"Wayne Elsey makes things happen. He sees a need and doesn't simply talk about it. He gets to work and addresses the need. I'm thankful he's penning some of his stories to encourage all of us to be better together. This book gives me even more hope for humanity." – **Ron Edmondson, CEO, Leadership Network**

"I've known Wayne since high school, and have had the privilege of becoming reacquainted over the last several years. He is a kind and generous man, not only financially generous but most importantly, he gives of himself. He is a straight shooter, and his sense of humor will keep you smiling. He searches for the good in everything and his energy for inspiring others is tireless. To me, his wealth is not measured by his bank account, but the size of his heart for humanity." – **Delia Phipps Mitchell, Long-Time Pal**

"I first met Wayne in 2009 while working for a nonprofit on a fourteen month nationwide fundraising campaign. I was desperate for ideas on how to be successful while navigating through the fundraising woes in the nonprofit world. Thankfully, a mutual friend told me to reach out to Wayne, so I did. He quickly invited me to his office and openly shared his story and desire to help others.

Wayne Elsey is what I commonly refer to as a 'Hope Dealer.' That is, he readily and freely loves to give hope to everyone he meets. He's a hard-working social entrepreneur that sees potential around every corner and in every person. He leads from a generous heart and writes from years of experience.

Thankfully, over the past ten years, Wayne has continued to be a mentor and friend. He has openly shared his heart and knowledge without hesitation. He also provided the inspiration I needed to keep on my pathway to hope and sharing it with others.

I'm thankful that he is now sharing that passion through his latest book, *Tied Together: A Pathway to Hope*. His writing will help you become a better leader and inspire you to do more to help others." – **Joe Wilson, Chief Development Officer, America World Adoption**

"It takes such little effort to look someone in the eyes, use both of your own ears to listen and truly convey appreciation for the little things others bless us with in our lives. Saying 'thank you' for big gifts is easy. Wayne Elsey gets this! In his newest book, Wayne stresses the importance of collaboration; why and how we don't need to 'go it alone.' He shares his own strength in the journey and proves that being inclusive and collaborative, work. I highly recommend you make this book a staple on your shelf as a go-to read for 2019." – **Wendy Lyn Phillips, President of CEA; CommunityEventApps.com, Author and Branding Strategist**

"Wayne has a way of reminding you of the notion that—in the midst of the constant distractions, the relentless noise, and the unforgiving challenges—you can choose to make a difference. You don't have to be a social entrepreneur, a priest, or even an activist to make a lasting impact in the world. You just need to believe that hope is more tangible, real, and attainable than it might seem most of the time. You already have what you need within you to do so—the power to choose. And Wayne reminds you always to choose hope." – **Ben Stroup, Author, Strategist, Executive**

"I started a nonprofit at a young age and was fortunate enough to meet Wayne when I was 14 years old. *Tied Together: A Pathway to Hope* captures the essence of Wayne's talent, and most of all, vision.

Our world today has evolved into a beautiful, but an also difficult place. Wayne's mission to bridge the gap between entrepreneurship and positive social impact is a beacon of hope, of light. As a pioneer of social entrepreneurship, Wayne is paving the way for an entirely new generation of entrepreneurs. Individuals who are inspired to better the world in which we live through their work, be it humanitarian, environmental or eradicating systemic poverty. With positive social impact in mind, Wayne is making the world a better place." **– Jacob Rice, Entrepreneur**

Made in the USA
Columbia, SC
02 July 2019